AESOP'S
FABLES

AESOP'S FABLES

From Translations of
Thomas James and George Tyler Townsend

With the Illustrations
of Grandville

THE FRANKLIN LIBRARY

Franklin Center, Pennsylvania

In 1838 the French political caricaturist Jean-Ignace Isidore Gérard (1803–1847), who worked under the pseudonym of Grandville, achieved lasting popularity for his illustrations to the *Fables* of La Fontaine. Like Aesop's fables, from which they were largely derived, La Fontaine's are a mirror of human vices, follies, and virtues, seen through talking animals. Grandville is considered one of the most outstanding of the many illustrators of these ancient fables because of his wry blending of human and animal features. His illustrations have been reproduced for this Franklin Library edition from a deluxe octavo volume of *Fables de La Fontaine* published by Garnier Frères, Libraires-Editeurs, Paris, during the mid-nineteenth century.

✧   ✧   ✧   ✧   ✧   ✧   ✧   ✧   ✧   ✧   ✧   ✧

CONTENTS

The Man, the Horse, the Ox, and the Dog

A Horse, an Ox, and a Dog, driven to great straits by the cold, sought shelter and protection from a Man. He received them kindly, lighted a fire, and warmed them. He made the Horse free of his oats, gave the Ox abundance of hay, and fed the Dog with meat from his own table. Grateful for these favors, they determined to repay him to the best of their ability. They divided for this purpose the term of his life between them, and each endowed one portion of it with the qualities which chiefly characterized himself. The Horse chose his earliest years, and endowed them with his own attributes: hence every man is in his youth impetuous, headstrong, and obstinate in maintaining his own opinion. The Ox took under his patronage the next term of life, and, therefore, man in his middle age is fond of work, devoted to labor, and resolute to amass wealth, and to husband his resources. The end of life was reserved to the Dog, wherefore an old man is often snappish, irritable, hard to please, and selfish; tolerant only of his own household, but averse to strangers, and to all who do not administer to his comfort or to his necessities.

The Hares and the Foxes

The Hares waged war with the Eagles, and called upon the Foxes to help them. The Foxes replied, "We would willingly have helped you, if we had not known who you were, and with whom you were fighting."

Count the cost before you commit yourselves.

The Miser

A Miser, to make sure of his property, sold all that he had and converted it into a great lump of gold, which he hid in a hole in the ground, and which he went continually to visit and inspect. This roused the curiosity of one of his workmen, who, suspecting that there was a treasure, when his master's back was turned went to the spot, and stole it away. When the Miser returned and found the place empty, he wept and tore his hair. But a neighbor who saw him in this extravagant grief, and learned the cause of it, said, "Fret yourself no longer, but take a stone and put it in the same place, and think that it is your lump of gold; for, as you never meant to use it, the one will do you as much good as the other."

The worth of money is not in its possession, but in its use.

The Lion, the Tiger, and the Fox

A Lion and a Tiger found the carcass of a Fawn, and had a long fight for it. The contest was so hard and even, that at last, both of them half-blinded and half-dead lay panting on the ground, without strength to touch the prize that was stretched between them. A Fox coming by at the time, and seeing their helpless condition, stepped in between the combatants and carried off the booty. "Poor creatures that we are," cried they, "who have been exhausting all our strength and injuring one another, merely to give a rogue a dinner!"

The Egret and the Arrow

A Bowman took aim at an Egret and hit him in the heart. As the Egret turned his head in the agony of death, he saw that the Arrow was winged with his own feathers. "How much sharper," said he, "are the wounds made by weapons which we ourselves have supplied!"

The Ass, the Fox,
and the Lion

An Ass and a Fox, having made an alliance, went out into the fields to hunt. On the way they met a Lion. The Fox, seeing the impending danger, made up to the Lion, and whispered that he would betray the Ass into the Lion's power, if he would promise to bear him harmless. The Lion having agreed to do so, the Fox contrived to lead the Ass into a snare. The Lion no sooner saw the Ass secured, than he fell at once upon the Fox, reserving the other for his next meal.

The Wolves
and the Sheep

Once on a time, the Wolves sent an embassy to the Sheep, desiring that there might be peace between them for the time to come. "Why," said they, "should we be forever waging this dreadful strife? Those wicked Dogs are the cause of all; they are incessantly barking at us, and provoking us. Send them away, and there will be no longer any obstacle to our eternal friendship and peace." The silly Sheep listened, the Dogs were dismissed, and the flock, thus deprived of their best protectors, became an easy prey to their treacherous enemy.

The Goat and the Goatherd

A Goat had strayed from the herd, and the Goatherd was trying all he could to bring him back to his companions. When by calling and whistling he could make no impression on him, at last, taking up a stone, he struck the Goat on the horn and broke it. Alarmed at what he had done, he besought the Goat not to tell his master, but the Goat replied, "O most foolish of Goatherds! my horn will tell the story, though I should not utter a word."

Facts speak plainer than words.

The Wolf and the Goat

A Wolf, seeing a Goat feeding on the brow of a high precipice where he could not come near her, besought her to come down lower, for fear she would miss her footing at that dizzy height. "Moreover," said he, "the grass is far sweeter and more abundant here below." But the Goat replied, "Excuse me; it is not for *my* dinner that you invite me, but for your own."

The Laborer
and the Snake

A Snake, having made his home close to the porch of a cottage, inflicted a severe bite on the Cottager's infant son, of which to the great grief of his parents he died. The father resolved to kill the Snake, and the next day, on its coming out of its hole for food, the Cottager took up his axe. But, making too much haste to hit him as he wriggled away, he missed his head, and cut off only the end of his tail. After some time, the Cottager, afraid lest the Snake should bite him also, endeavored to make peace, and placed some bread and salt in his hole. The Snake, hissing slightly, said, "There can henceforth be no peace between us; for whenever I see you I shall remember the loss of my tail, and whenever you see me you will be thinking of the death of your son."

No one truly forgets injuries in the presence of him who caused the injury.

The Quack Frog

A Frog emerging from the mud of a swamp, proclaimed to all the world that he was come to cure all diseases. "Here!" he cried, "come and see a doctor, the proprietor of medicines such as man never heard of before, no, not even Aesculapius himself, Jove's court-physician!" "And how," said the Fox, "dare you set up to heal others, who are not able to cure your own limping gait, and blotched and wrinkled skin?"

The Countryman
and the Snake

A Countryman returning home one winter's day, found a Snake by the hedgeside, half dead with cold. Taking compassion on the creature, he laid it in his bosom, and brought it home to his fireside, to revive it. No sooner had the warmth restored it, than it began to attack the children of the cottage. Upon this the Countryman, whose compassion had saved its life, took up a pick and laid the Snake dead at his feet.

Those who return evil for good, may expect their neighbor's pity to be worn out at last.

The Crow and the Raven

A Crow was very jealous of the Raven, because he was considered a bird of good omen, and always attracted the attention of men, as indicating by his flight the good or evil course of future events. Seeing some travellers approaching, the Crow flew up into a tree, and perching herself on one of the branches, cawed as loudly as she could. The travellers turned towards the sound, and wondered what it boded, when one of them said to his companion, "Let us proceed on our journey, my friend, for it is only the caw of a Crow, and her cry, you know, is no omen."

Those who assume a character which does not belong to them, only make themselves ridiculous.

The Camel

When Men first saw the Camel, they were so frightened at his vast size that they fled away. After a time, perceiving the meekness and gentleness of the Camel's temper, they summoned courage enough to approach him. Soon afterwards, observing that he was an animal altogether deficient in spirit, they assumed such boldness as to put a bridle in his mouth, and to set a child to drive him.

The Wolf
and the Shepherds

A Wolf looking into a hut and seeing some Shepherds comfortably regaling themselves on a joint of mutton—"A pretty row," said he, "would these men have made if they had caught me at such a supper!"

Men are too apt to condemn in others the very things that they practise themselves.

The Dog and the Shadow

A Dog had stolen a piece of meat out of a butcher's shop, and was crossing a river on his way home, when he saw his own shadow reflected in the stream below. Thinking that it was another dog with another piece of meat, he resolved to make himself master of that also, but in snapping at the supposed treasure, he dropped the bit he was carrying, and so lost all.

Those who grasp at the shadow are likely to lose the substance.

Hercules
and the Wagoner

As a Countryman was carelessly driving his wagon along a muddy lane, his wheels stuck so deep in the clay that the horses came to a standstill. Upon this the Countryman, without making the least effort of his own, began to call upon Hercules to come and help him out of his trouble. But Hercules bade him lay his shoulder to the wheel, assuring him that Heaven aided only those who endeavored to help themselves.

It is in vain to expect our prayers to be heard, if we do not strive as well as pray.

The Monkey and the Fishermen

A Monkey was sitting up in a high tree, when he saw some Fishermen laying their nets in a river. The Men had no sooner set their nets, and retired a short distance to their dinner, than the Monkey came down from the tree, thinking that he would try his hand at the same sport. But in attempting to lay the nets he got so entangled in them, that, being well nigh choked, he was forced to exclaim: "This serves me right. For what business had I, who know nothing of fishing, to meddle with such tackle as this?"

The Husbandman
and the Sea

A Husbandman, seeing a ship full of sailors tossed about up and down upon the billows, cried out, "O Sea! Thou art a deceitful and pitiless element, that destroyest all who venture upon thee!" The Sea heard him, and assuming a woman's voice replied, "Do not reproach me; I am not the cause of this disturbance, but the Winds, that when they fall upon me will give no repose. But should you sail over me when they are away, you will say that I am milder and more tractable than your own mother earth."

The Olive Tree
and the Fig Tree

The Olive tree ridiculed the Fig tree because, while she was green all the year round, the Fig tree changed its leaves with the seasons. A shower of snow fell upon them, and, finding the Olive full of foliage, the snow settled upon its branches, and, bearing them down with its weight, at once despoiled it of its beauty and killed the tree. But finding the Fig tree denuded of leaves, the snow fell through to the ground, and did not injure it at all.

The Farmer
and His Two Daughters

A Man who had two daughters married one to a Gardener, the other to a Potter. After a while he paid a visit to the Gardener's, and asked his daughter how she was, and how it fared with her. "Excellently well," said she, "we have everything that we want. I have but one prayer: that we may have a heavy storm of rain to water our plants." Off he set to the Potter's, and asked his other daughter how matters went with her. "There is not a thing we want," she replied; "and I only hope this fine weather and hot sun may continue, to bake our tiles." "Alack," said the Father, "if you wish for fine weather, and your sister for rain, which am I to pray for?"

The Dolphins
and the Herring

The Dolphins and the Whales were at war with one another, and while the battle was at its height the Herring stepped in and endeavored to separate them. But one of the Dolphins cried out, "Let us alone, friend! We had rather perish in the contest, than be reconciled by you."

The Lion
and the Dolphin

A Lion was roaring on the seashore, when, seeing a Dolphin basking on the surface of the water, he invited him to form an alliance with him. "For," said he, "as I am the King of the Beasts, and you are the King of the Fishes, we ought to be the greatest friends and allies possible." The Dolphin gladly assented, and the Lion, not long after, having a fight with a wild bull, called upon the Dolphin for his promised support. But when the Dolphin, though ready to assist him, found himself unable to come out of the sea for the purpose, the Lion accused him of having betrayed him. "Do not blame me," said the Dolphin in reply, "but blame my nature, which however powerful at sea, is altogether helpless on land."

The Swan and the Goose

A certain rich man bought a Goose and a Swan in the market. He fed the one for his table, and kept the other for the sake of its song. When the time came for killing the Goose, the cook went to take him at night, when it was dark, and he was not able to distinguish one bird from the other. In the darkness he caught the Swan instead of the Goose. The Swan, threatened with death, burst forth into song, and thus made himself known by his voice, and so preserved his life.

A word in season is most precious.

The Hunter
and the Woodsman

A not very bold Hunter was searching for the tracks of a Lion. He asked a man felling oaks if he had seen any of the Lion's tracks or if he knew where his lair was. "Yes," said the Man, "and if you will come with me I will show you the Lion himself." At this the Hunter, turning ghastly pale, and his teeth chattering, said, "Oh, thank you; it was the Lion's tracks, not himself, that I was hunting."

A coward can be a hero at a distance; it is presence of danger that tests the presence of mind.

The Creaking Wheels

As some Oxen were dragging a wagon along a heavy road, the Wheels set up a tremendous creaking. "Brute!" cried the driver to the wagon, "why do you groan, when they who are drawing all the weight are silent?"

Those who cry loudest are not always the most hurt.

The Lion, the Wolf, and the Fox

A Lion, growing old, lay sick in his cave. All the beasts came to visit their king, except the Fox. The Wolf, therefore, thinking that he had a capital opportunity, accused the Fox to the Lion of not paying any respect to him who had the rule over them all, and of not coming to visit him. At that very moment the Fox came in, and heard these last words of the Wolf. As the Lion roared out in a rage against him, the Fox sought an opportunity to defend himself, and said, "And who of all those who have come to you, have benefited you so much as I, who have travelled from place to place in every direction, and have sought and learnt from the physicians, the means of healing you?" The Lion commanded him immediately to tell him the cure, and the Fox replied, "You must flay a wolf alive, and wrap his skin, yet warm, around you." The Wolf was at once taken and flayed, whereon the Fox, turning to him, said, with a smile, "You should have moved your master not to ill, but to good will."

Jupiter and the Camel

When the Camel, in days of yore, besought Jupiter to grant him horns, for it was a great grief to him to see other animals furnished with them, while he had none, Jupiter not only refused to give him the horns he asked for, but cropped his ears short for his importunity.

By asking too much, we may lose the little that we have.

The Vine and the Goat

There was a Vine teeming with ripe fruit and tender shoots, when a wanton Goat came up and gnawed the bark, and browsed upon the young leaves. "I will revenge myself on you," said the Vine, "for this insult. For when in a few days you are brought as a victim to the altar, the juice of my grapes shall be the dew of death upon thy forehead."

Retribution though late comes at last.

The Wolf and the Shepherd

A Wolf had long hung about a flock of sheep, and had done them no harm. The Shepherd, however, had his suspicions, and for a while was always on the lookout against him as an avowed enemy. But when the Wolf continued for a long time following in the train of his flock without the least attempt to annoy them, the Shepherd began to look upon him more as a friend than a foe; and having one day occasion to go into the city, he intrusted the sheep to his care. The Wolf no sooner saw his opportunity, than he forthwith fell upon the sheep and destroyed them. The Shepherd, on his return, seeing his flock destroyed, exclaimed, "Fool that I am! yet I deserved no less for trusting my Sheep with a Wolf!"

There is more danger from a pretended friend than from an open enemy.

The Jackass in Office

An Ass carrying an Image in a religious procession was driven through a town, and all the people whom it passed made reverent bows. Upon this, the Ass, supposing that they intended this worship for himself, was mightily puffed up, and would not budge another step. But the driver soon laid the stick across his back, saying at the same time, "You silly dolt! it is not you that they revere, but the Image which you carry."

The Dog's House

A Dog who spent his winters rolled together and coiled up in as small a space as possible on account of the cold, determined to make himself a house. When the summer returned again he spent his time dozing, stretched at his full length, and thought himself a very big dog indeed, and considered, furthermore, that it would be neither an easy nor a necessary work to make himself such a house as would accommodate him.

The Birdcatcher and the Lark

A Birdcatcher was setting springs upon a common, when a Lark, who saw him at work, asked him from a distance what he was doing. "I am establishing a colony," said he, "and laying the foundations of my first city." Upon that, the man retired to a little distance and hid himself. The Lark, believing his assertion, soon flew down to the place, and swallowing the bait, found himself entangled in the noose; whereupon the Birdcatcher straightway coming up to him, made him his prisoner. "A pretty fellow are you!" said the Lark. "If these are the colonies you found, you will not find many immigrants."

The Oak
and the Woodcutters

The Woodcutters cut down a Mountain Oak, split it in pieces, making wedges of its own branches for dividing the trunk, and for saving their labor. The Oak said with a sigh, "I do not care about the blows of the axe aimed at my roots, but I do grieve at being torn in pieces by these wedges made from my own branches."

Misfortunes springing from ourselves are the hardest to bear.

The Fox and the Goat

A Fox had fallen into a well, and had been casting about for a long time how he should get out again, when at length a Goat came to the place and, wanting to drink, asked him whether the water was good, and if there was plenty of it. The Fox, dissembling the real danger of his case, replied, "Come down, my friend. The water is so good that I cannot drink enough of it, and so abundant that it cannot be exhausted." Upon this the Goat without any more ado leaped in, but after satisfying his thirst, he asked the Fox how they were to get out of the well. The Fox replied that it would be quite simple if they helped each other. "If you will rear up and place your front feet against the side of the well and bend your horns forward, I can easily mount on your back and climb out." The Goat did as he was told and the Fox nimbly climbed up his back and with one jump from the Goat's horns, was safely out of the well. "Now it is your turn to help me out," said the Goat. But the Fox, leaving him in the lurch, called back, "My friend, if you had half as much brains as you have beard, you would have looked before you leaped."

The Wolf and the Lion

One day a Wolf had seized a sheep from a fold, and was carrying it home to his own den, when he met a Lion, who straightway laid hold of the sheep and bore it away. The Wolf, standing at a distance, cried out that it was a great shame, and that the Lion had robbed him of his own. The Lion laughed, and said, "I suppose, then, that it was your good friend the shepherd who gave it to *you*."

The Owl and the Birds

An Owl, in her wisdom, counselled the Birds, when the acorn first began to sprout, to pull it up out of the ground, and not to allow it to grow, because it would produce the mistletoe, from which an irremediable poison, the birdlime, would be extracted, and by which they would be captured. The Owl next advised them to pluck up the seed of the flax, which men had sown, as it was a plant which boded no good to them, for nets would be made from it. And, lastly, the Owl, seeing an archer approach, predicted that this man, being on foot, would contrive darts armed with feathers, which should fly faster than the wings of the birds themselves. The Birds gave no credence to these warning words, but considered the Owl to be beside herself, and said that she was mad. But afterwards, finding her words were true, they wondered at her knowledge, and deemed her to be the wisest of birds. Hence it is that when she appears they resort to her as knowing all things, while she no longer gives them advice, but in solitude laments their past folly.

The Collier
and the Fuller

A Collier, who had more room in his house than he wanted for himself, proposed to a Fuller to come and take up his quarters with him. "Thank you," said the Fuller, "but I must decline your offer, for I fear that as fast as I whiten my goods you will blacken them again."

The Thirsty Pigeon

A Pigeon sorely pressed by thirst, saw a glass of water painted upon a sign. Supposing it to be real, she dashed down at it with all her might. She struck the board, and, breaking her wing, fell helpless to the ground, where she was quickly captured by one of the passersby.

Great haste is not always good speed.

The Ass
and His Purchaser

A Man wished to purchase an Ass, and agreed with its owner that he should try him before he bought him. He took the Ass home, and put him in the strawyard with his other Asses, upon which the Ass left all the others, and joined himself at once to the most idle, and the greatest eater of them all. The man, seeing this, put a halter on him, and led him back to his owner. On his inquiring how, in so short a time, he could have made a trial of him: "I do not need a trial," he answered, "I know that he will be just the same as the one whom, of all the rest, he chose for his companion."

A man is known by the company he keeps.

The Lion and the Goat

On a summer's day, when everything was suffering from extreme heat, a Lion and a Goat came at the same time to quench their thirst at a small fountain. They at once fell to quarrelling which should first drink the water, until at length it appeared that each was determined to resist the other even to death. But, ceasing from the strife for a moment, to re-cover their breath, they saw a flock of vultures hovering over them, only waiting to pounce upon whichever of them should fall. Whereupon they instantly made up their quarrel, agreeing that it was far better for them both to become friends, than to furnish food for the crows and vultures.

The Horse and the Stag

A Horse had the whole range of a meadow to himself; but a Stag came and damaged the pasture. The Horse, anxious to have his revenge, asked a Man if he could not assist him in punishing the Stag. "Yes," said the Man, "only let me put a bit in your mouth, and get upon your back, and I will find the weapons." The Horse agreed, and the Man mounted accordingly; but instead of getting his revenge, the Horse has been from that time forward the slave of Man.

Revenge is too dearly purchased at the price of liberty.

The Rivers and the Sea

Once upon a time the Rivers combined against the Sea, and, going in a body, accused her, saying, "Why is it that when we Rivers pour our waters into you so fresh and sweet, you straightway render them salt and unpalatable?" The Sea, observing the temper in which they came, merely answered, "If you do not wish to become salt, please keep away from me altogether."

The Philosopher,
the Ants, and Mercury

A Philosopher witnessed from the shore the shipwreck of a vessel, the crew and passengers of which were all drowned. He inveighed against the injustice of Providence, which would for the sake of one criminal, perchance sailing in the ship, allow so many innocent persons to perish. As he was indulging in these reflections, he found himself surrounded by a whole army of Ants, near to whose nest he was standing. One of them climbed up and stung him, and he immediately trampled them all to death with his foot. Mercury presented himself, and striking the Philosopher with his wand, said, "And are you indeed to make yourself a judge of the dealings of Providence, who hast thyself in a similar manner treated these poor Ants?"

The same measures will not suit all circumstances; and we may play the same trick once too often.

The Hound and the Hare

A Hound, after long chasing a Hare, at last came up to her, and kept first biting and then licking her. The Hare, not knowing what to make of him, said, "If you are a friend, why do you bite me?—but if a foe, why caress me?"

A doubtful friend is worse than a certain enemy. Let a man be one thing or the other, and we then know how to meet him.

The Widow
and the Sheep

There was a certain Widow who had only one Sheep, and, wishing to make the most of his wool, she sheared him so closely that she cut his skin as well as his fleece. The Sheep, smarting under this treatment, cried out: "Why do you torture me thus? What will my blood add to the weight of the wool? If you want my flesh, Dame, send for the Butcher, who will put me out of my misery at once, but if you want my fleece, send for the Shearer, who will clip my wool without drawing my blood."

Middle measures are often but middling measures.

The Kid and the Wolf

A Kid that had strayed from the herd was pursued by a Wolf. When she saw all other hope of escape was cut off, she turned to the Wolf and said, "I must allow indeed that I am your victim, but as my life is now but short, let it be merry. Do you pipe for a while, and I will dance." While the Wolf was piping and the Kid was dancing, the Dogs hearing the music ran up to see what was going on, and the Wolf was glad to take himself off as fast as his legs would carry him.

He who steps out of his way to play the fool, must not wonder if he misses the prize.

The Lion and the Mouse

A Lion was sleeping in his lair, when a Mouse, not knowing where he was going, ran over the mighty beast's nose and awakened him. The Lion clapped his paw upon the frightened little creature, and was about to make an end of him in a moment, when the Mouse, in pitiable tones, besought him to spare one who had so unconsciously offended, and not stain his honorable paws with so insignificant a prey. The Lion, smiling at his little prisoner's fright, generously let him go. Now it happened a short time after, that the Lion, while ranging the woods for his prey, fell into the coils of the hunters and, finding himself entangled without hope of escape, set up a roar that filled the whole forest with its echo. The Mouse, recognizing the voice of his former preserver, ran to the spot, and without more ado set to work to nibble the knot in the cord that bound the Lion, and in a short time set the noble beast at liberty; thus convincing him that kindness is seldom thrown away, and that there is no creature so much below another but that he may have it in his power to return a good office.

The Travellers
and the Bear

Two friends were travelling on the same road together, when they met with a Bear. One of them in great fear, without a thought of his companion, climbed up into a tree, and hid himself. The other, seeing that he had no chance, single-handed, against the Bear, had nothing left but to throw himself on the ground and feign to be dead; for he had heard that a Bear will never touch a dead body. As he lay thus, the Bear came up to his head, muzzling and snuffing at his nose, and ears, and heart, but the man immovably held his breath, and the beast supposing him to be dead, walked away. When the Bear was fairly out of sight, his companion came down out of the tree, and asked what it was that the Bear had whispered to him—"for," said he, "I observed he put his mouth very close to your ear." "Why," replied the other, "it was no great secret; he only bade me have a care how I keep company with those who, when they get into a difficulty, leave their friends in the lurch."

The Flea and the Wrestler

A Flea settled upon the bare foot of a Wrestler, and bit him; on which he called loudly upon Hercules for help. The Flea a second time hopped upon his foot, when the Wrestler groaned and said, "O Hercules! if you do not help me against a Flea, how can I hope for your assistance against great antagonists?"

The Sick Lion

A Lion, no longer able, from the weakness of old age, to hunt for his prey, laid himself up in his den, and, breathing with great difficulty, and speaking with a low voice, gave out that he was very ill indeed. The report soon spread among the beasts, and there was great lamentation for the sick Lion. One beast after another came to see him, but catching them thus alone and in his own den, the Lion made an easy prey of them, and grew fat upon his diet. The Fox, suspecting the truth of the matter, came at length to make his visit of inquiry, and standing at some distance, asked his Majesty how he did. "Ah, my dearest friend," said the Lion, "is it you? Why do you stand so far from me? Come, sweet friend, and pour a word of consolation in the poor Lion's ear, who has but a short time to live." "Bless you!" said the Fox, "but excuse me if I cannot stay. For, to tell the truth, I feel quite uneasy at the mark of the footsteps that I see here, all pointing towards your den, and none returning outwards."

Affairs are easier of entrance than of exit, and it is but common prudence to see our way out before we venture in.

The Fisherman

A Fisherman went to a river to fish. When he had laid his nets across the stream, he tied a stone to a long cord, and beat the water on either side of the net, to drive the fish into the meshes. One of his neighbors who lived nearby, seeing him thus employed, went up to him and blamed him exceedingly for disturbing the water, and making it so muddy as to be unfit to drink. "I am sorry," said the Fisherman, "that this does not please you, but it is by thus troubling the waters that I gain my living."

The Lion and the Bulls

Three Bulls fed in a field together in the greatest peace and amity. A Lion had long watched them in the hope of making a prize of them, but found that there was little chance for him so long as they all kept together. He, therefore, began secretly to spread evil and slanderous reports of one against the other, till he had fomented a jealousy and distrust amongst them. No sooner did the Lion see that they avoided one another, and fed each by himself apart, than he fell upon them singly, and so made an easy prey of them all.

The quarrels of friends are the opportunities of foes.

The Dancing Monkeys

A Prince had some Monkeys trained to dance. Being naturally great mimics of men's actions, they showed themselves most apt pupils; and, when arrayed in their rich clothes and masks, they danced as well as any of the courtiers. The spectacle was often repeated with great applause, till on one occasion a courtier, bent on mischief, took from his pocket a handful of nuts, and threw them upon the stage. The Monkeys, at the sight of the nuts, forgot their dancing, and became (as indeed they were) Monkeys instead of actors, and, pulling off their masks and tearing their robes, they fought with one another for the nuts. The dancing spectacle thus came to an end, amidst the laughter and ridicule of the audience.

The Swollen Fox

A Fox, very much famished, and seeing some bread and meat left by shepherds in the hollow of an oak, crept into the hole and made a hearty meal. When he finished, he was so full that he was not able to get out, and began to groan and lament very sadly. Another Fox passing by, heard his cries, and coming up, inquired the cause of his complaining. On learning what had happened, he said to him, "Ah, you will have to remain there, my friend, until you become such as you were when you crept in, and then you will easily get out."

The Seaside Travellers

As some Travellers were making their way along the seashore, they came to a cliff, and looking out upon the sea saw a Faggot floating at a distance, which they thought at first must be a large Ship, so they waited, expecting to see it come into harbor. As the

Faggot drifted nearer to shore, they thought it no longer to be a Ship, but a Boat. But when it was at length thrown on the beach, they saw that it was nothing but a Faggot after all.

Dangers seem greatest at a distance, and coming events are magnified according to the interest or inclination of the beholder.

The Fawn and His Mother

A young Fawn once said to his mother, "You are larger than a dog, and swifter, and more used to running, and you also have your horns as a defense. Why then, O Mother! are you always in such terrible fright of the hounds?" She smiled and said, "I know full well, my son, that all you say is true. I have the advantages you mention, but yet when I hear only the bark of a single dog I feel ready to faint, and fly away as fast as I can."

No arguments will give courage to a coward.

The Eagle and the Beetle

A Hare, being chased by an Eagle, betook himself for refuge to the nest of a Beetle, whom he entreated to save him. The Beetle, therefore, interceded with the Eagle, begging of him not to kill the poor suppliant, and conjuring him by mighty Jupiter not to slight his intercession and break the laws of hospitality because he was so small an animal. But the Eagle, in wrath, gave the Beetle a flap with his wing, and straightway seized upon the Hare and devoured him. When the Eagle flew away, the Beetle flew after him to learn where his nest was and, getting into it, he rolled the Eagle's eggs out of it one by one, and broke them. The Eagle, grieved and enraged to think that any one should attempt so audacious a thing, built his nest the next time in a higher place, but there too the Beetle got at it again, and served him in the same manner as before. Upon this the Eagle, being at a loss as to what to do, flew up to Jupiter, his Lord and King, and placed the third brood of eggs, as a sacred deposit, in his lap, begging him to guard them for him. But the Beetle, having made a little ball of dirt, flew up with it and dropped it in Jupiter's lap; who, rising up on a sudden to shake it off, and forgetting the eggs, threw them

down, and they were again broken. Jupiter being informed by the Beetle that he had done this to be revenged upon the Eagle, who had not only wronged him, but had acted impiously towards Jove himself, told the Eagle, when he came to him, that the Beetle was the aggrieved party, and that he complained not without reason. But being unwilling that the race of Eagles should be diminished, he advised the Beetle to come to an accommodation with the Eagle. As the Beetle would not agree to this, Jupiter transferred the Eagle's breeding to another season, when there are no Beetles to be seen.

No one can slight the laws of hospitality with impunity, and there is no station or influence, however powerful, that can protect the oppressor, in the end, from the vengeance of the oppressed.

The Ant and the Dove

An Ant went to a fountain to quench his thirst, and tumbling in, was almost drowned. But a Dove that happened to be sitting on a neighboring tree saw the

Ant's danger, and plucking off a leaf, let it drop into the water before him, and the Ant, mounting upon it, was presently wafted safely ashore. Just at that time, a Fowler was spreading his net, and was in the act of ensnaring the Dove, when the Ant, perceiving his object, bit his heel. The start which the man gave made him drop his net, and the Dove, aroused to a sense of her danger, flew safely away.

One good turn deserves another.

The Dogs and the Hides

Some hungry Dogs, seeing some raw Hides which a skinner had left in the bottom of a stream, and not being able to reach them, agreed among themselves to drink up the river to get at the prize. So they set to work, but they all burst themselves with drinking before ever they came near the Hides.

Those who aim at an object by unreasonable means, are apt to ruin themselves in the attempt.

The Bold Kid
and the Wolf

A Kid, being mounted on the roof of a lofty house and seeing a Wolf pass below, began to revile him. The Wolf merely stopped to reply, "Coward! It is not you who revile me, but the place on which you are standing."

Time and place often give the advantage to the weak over the strong.

Jupiter, Neptune,
Minerva, and Momus

Jupiter, Neptune, and Minerva (as the story goes) once contended which of them should make the most perfect thing. Jupiter made a Man, Pallas made a House, Neptune made a Bull, and Momus—for he had not yet been turned out of Olympus—was chosen to judge which production had the greatest merit. He began by finding fault with the Bull, because his horns were not below his eyes, so that he might see when he butted with them. Next he found fault with the Man, because there was no window in his breast that all might see his inward thoughts and feelings. And lastly he found fault with the House, because it had no wheels to enable its inhabitants to remove from bad neighbors. But Jupiter forthwith drove the critic out of heaven, telling him that a fault-finder could never be pleased, and that it was time to criticize the works of others when he had done some good thing himself.

The Cock and the Jewel

A Cock, scratching for some food for himself and his hens, found a precious stone to which he said, "If your owner had found thee and not I, he would have taken thee up and have thee set in precious metal, befitting your value. I have found thee for no purpose. I would rather have one barleycorn than all the jewels in the world."

The Hart and the Vine

A Hart, chased by Hunters, concealed himself among the branches of a Vine. The Hunters passed by without discovering him, and when he thought that all was safe, he began browsing upon the leaves that had concealed him. But one of the Hunters, attracted by the rustling, turned round, and, guessing that their prey was there, shot into the bush and killed him. As he was dying, he groaned out these words: "I suffer justly for my ingratitude, who could not forbear injuring the Vine that had protected me in time of danger."

The Lion, Jupiter,
and the Elephant

The Lion wearied Jupiter with his frequent complaints. "It is true," he said, "O Jupiter! that I am gigantic in strength, handsome in shape, and powerful in attack. I have jaws well provided with teeth, and feet furnished with claws, and I lord it over all the beasts of the forest. What a disgrace it is, that being such as I am, I should be frightened by the crowing of a cock." Jupiter replied, "Why do you blame me, and without a cause? I have given you all the attributes which I possess myself, and your courage never fails you except in this one instance." On this the Lion groaned and lamented very much, and reproached himself with his cowardice, and wished that he might die. As these thoughts passed through his mind, he met an Elephant, and came near to hold a conversation with him. After a time he observed that the Elephant shook his ears very often, and he inquired what was the matter, and why his ears moved with such a tremor every now and then. Just at that moment a gnat settled on the head of the Elephant, and the Elephant replied, "Do you see that little buzzing insect? If it enters my ear, my fate is sealed. I should die presently." The Lion said, "Well, since so huge a beast is afraid of a tiny gnat, I will no more complain, nor wish myself dead. I find myself, even as I am, better off than the Elephant, in that very same degree that a cock is greater than a gnat."

Jupiter and the Bee

In days of old, when the world was young, a Bee that had stored her combs with a bountiful harvest, flew up to heaven to present as a sacrifice an offering of honey. Jupiter was so delighted with the gift, that he promised to give her whatsoever she should ask for. She therefore besought him, saying, "O glorious Jove, maker and master of me, poor Bee, give thy servant a sting, that when any one approaches my hive to take the honey, I will kill him on the spot." Jupiter, out of love to man, was angry at her request, and thus answered her: "Your prayer shall not be granted in the way you wish, but the sting which you ask for you shall have; and when any one comes to take away your honey and you attack him, the wound shall be fatal not to him but to you, for your life shall go with your sting."

The Crab
and Her Mother

Said an old Crab to a young one, "Why do you walk so crooked, child? Walk straight!" "Mother," said the young Crab, "show me the way, will you? and when I see you taking a straight course, I will try and follow."

Example is better than precept.

The Bald Knight

A certain Knight grew old, his hair fell off, and he became bald; to hide which imperfection he wore a periwig. But as he was riding out with some others, on a hunting expedition, a sudden gust of wind blew off the periwig, and exposed his bald pate. The company could not forbear laughing at the accident; and he himself laughed as loud as anybody, saying, "How was it to be expected that I should keep strange hair upon my head, when my own would not stay there?"

The Mice and the Weasels

The Mice and the Weasels had long been at war with each other. The Mice being worsted in battle, at length agreed at a meeting, solemnly called for the occasion, that their defeat was attributable to nothing but their want of discipline, and they determined accordingly to elect regular commanders for the time to come. So they chose those whose valor and prowess most recommended them to the important post. The new commanders, proud of their position, and desirous of being as conspicuous as possible, bound horns upon their foreheads as a sort of crest and mark of distinction. Not long after, a battle ensued. The Mice, as before, were soon put to flight. The common herd escaped into their holes, but the commanders, not being able to get in from the length of their horns, were every one caught and devoured.

The Fox
and the Hedgehog

A Fox, while crossing over a river, was driven by the force of the stream into a narrow gorge, and lay there for a long time unable to get out, covered with myriads of horseflies that had fastened themselves upon him. A Hedgehog, who was wandering in that direction, saw him, and, taking compassion on him, asked him if he should drive away the flies that were so tormenting him. But the Fox begged him to do nothing of the sort. "Why not?" asked the Hedgehog. "Because," replied the Fox, "these flies that are upon me now, are already full, and draw but little blood, but should you remove them, a swarm of fresh and hungry ones will come, who will not leave a drop of blood in my body."

When we throw off rulers or dependents, who have already made the most of us, we do but lay ourselves open to others who will make us bleed more freely.

The Old Woman
and the Physician

An old Woman, who had become blind, called in a Physician, and promised him, before witnesses, that if he would restore her eyesight, she would give him a most handsome reward, but that if he did not cure her, and her malady remained, he should receive nothing. The agreement being concluded, the Physician tampered from time to time with the old lady's eyes, and meanwhile, bit by bit, carried off her goods. After a time, he set about the task in earnest and cured her, and thereupon asked for the stipulated fee. But the old Woman, on recovering her sight, saw none of her goods left in the house. When, therefore, the Physician importuned her in vain for payment, and she continually put him off with excuses, he summoned her at last before the Judges. Being now called upon for her defense, she said, "What this man says is true enough. I promised to give him his fee if my sight were restored, and nothing if my eyes continued bad. Now he says that I am cured, but I say just the contrary; for when my malady first came on, I could see all sorts of furniture and goods in my house, but now, when he says he has restored my sight, I cannot see one jot of either."

He who plays a trick must be prepared to take a joke.

The Doctor and His Patient

A Doctor had been for some time attending upon a sick Man, who, however, died under his hands. At the funeral the Doctor went about among the relations, saying, "Our poor friend, if he had only refrained from wine, and attended to his inside, and used proper means, would not have been lying there." One of the mourners answered him, "My good sir, it is of no use your saying this now. You ought to have prescribed these things when your Patient was alive to take them."

The best advice often comes too late.

The Mule

A Mule that had grown fat and wanton on too good an allowance of corn, was one day jumping and kicking about, and at length, cocking up her tail, exclaimed, "My dam was a Racer, and I am quite as good as ever she was." But being soon exhausted by her galloping and frisking, she remembered all at once that her sire was an Ass.

Every truth has two sides; it is well to look at both, before we commit ourselves to either.

The Lion and the Ass
Go Hunting

A Lion and an Ass made an agreement to go out hunting together. By-and-by they came to a cave, where many wild goats were living. The Lion took up his station at the mouth of the cave, and the Ass, going within, kicked and brayed and made a mighty fuss to frighten them out. When the Lion had caught very many of them, the Ass came out and asked him if he had not made a noble fight, and routed the goats properly. "Yes, indeed," said the Lion, "and I assure you, you would have frightened me too, if I had not known you to be an Ass."

When braggarts are admitted into the company of their betters, it is only to be made use of, or be laughed at.

The Two Pots

Two Pots, one of earthenware, the other of brass, were carried down a river in a flood. The Brazen Pot begged his companion to keep by his side, and he would protect him. "Thank you for your offer," said the Earthen Pot, "but that is just what I'm afraid of. If you will only keep at a distance, I may float down in safety, but should we come in contact, I am sure to be the sufferer."

Avoid too powerful neighbors, for, should there be a collision, the weakest goes to the wall.

The Farthing Rushlight

A Rushlight that had grown fat and saucy with too much grease, boasted one evening before a large company, that it shone brighter than the sun, the moon, and all the stars. At that moment a puff of wind came and blew it out. One who lighted it again said, "Shine on, friend Rushlight, and hold your tongue; the lights of heaven are never blown out."

The Heifer and the Ox

A Heifer that ran wild in the fields and never felt the yoke, upbraided an Ox at plough for submitting to such labor and drudgery. The Ox said nothing, but went on with his work. Not long after, there was a great festival. The Ox got his holiday, but the Heifer was led off to be sacrificed at the altar. "If this be the end of your idleness," said the Ox, "I think that my work is better than your play. I had rather my neck felt the yoke than the axe."

The Ass Carrying Salt

A certain Huckster who kept an Ass, hearing that Salt was to be had cheap at the seaside, drove down his Ass thither to buy some. Having loaded the beast with as much as he could bear, he was driving him home, when, as they were passing a slippery ledge of rock, the Ass fell into the stream below. The Salt being melted, the Ass was relieved of his burden, and having gained the bank with ease, pursued his journey onward, light in body and in spirit. The Huckster soon afterwards set off for the seashore for some more Salt, and loaded the Ass, if possible, yet more heavily than before. On their return, as they crossed the stream into which he had formerly fallen, the Ass fell down on purpose, and by the dissolving of the Salt was again released from his load. The Master, provoked at the loss, and thinking how he might cure him of this trick, on his next journey to the coast freighted the beast with a load of sponges. When they arrived at the same stream as before, the Ass was at his old tricks again, and rolled himself into the water. But the sponges becoming thoroughly wet, he found to his cost, as he proceeded homewards, that instead of lightening his burden, he had more than doubled its weight.

The Tortoise
and the Hare

A Hare jeered at a Tortoise for the slowness of his pace. The Tortoise laughed and said that he would be happy to run against her on any day she should name. "Come on," said the Hare, "and you shall see what my feet are made of." So it was agreed that they should start at once. The Tortoise started off at his steady pace, never pausing for a moment. The Hare, treating the whole matter very lightly, decided to take a short nap, confident that she would soon overtake the plodding Tortoise. Meanwhile the Tortoise continued on, never looking back, and never letting herself become distracted. When the Hare awoke it was far too late to win the race. The Tortoise had arrived at the goal long before.

Slow and steady wins the race.

The Ass and the Lapdog

There was an Ass and a Lapdog that belonged to one master. The Ass was tied up in the stable, and had plenty of corn and hay to eat, and was as well off as an Ass could be. The little Dog was always sporting and gambolling about, caressing and fawning upon his master in a thousand amusing ways, so that he became a great favorite, and was permitted to lie in his master's lap. The Ass, indeed, had enough to do; he was drawing wood all day, and had to take his turn at the mill at night. But while he grieved over his own lot, it galled him more and more to see the Lapdog living in such ease and luxury. So, thinking that if he acted like a pet to his master, he should fare the same, he broke one day from his halter, and rushing into the hall began to kick and prance about in the strangest fashion. Then, swishing his tail and mimicking the frolics of the favorite, he upset the table where his master was at dinner, breaking it in two and smashing all the crockery. Nor would he leave off till he jumped upon his master, and pawed him with his rough-shod feet. The servants, seeing their master in no little danger, thought it was now high time to interfere, and having released him from the Ass's caresses, they so belabored the silly creature with sticks and staves, that he never got up again, and as he breathed his last, he exclaimed, "Why could not I have been satisfied with my natural position, without attempting, by tricks and grimaces, to imitate one who was but a puppy after all!"

The Gamecocks and the Partridge

A Man had two Gamecocks in his poultry yard. One day by chance he fell in with a tame Partridge for sale. He purchased it, and brought it home that it might be reared with his Gamecocks. On its being put into the poultry yard they struck at it, and followed it about, so that the Partridge was grievously troubled in mind, and supposed that he was thus evilly treated because he was a stranger. Not long afterwards he saw the Cocks fighting together, and not separating before one had well beaten the other. He then said to himself, "I shall no longer distress myself at being struck at by these Gamecocks, when I see that they cannot even refrain from quarrelling with each other."

The Porker
and the Sheep

A young Porker took up his quarters in a fold of Sheep. One day the shepherd laid hold of him, and he squeaked and struggled with all his might and main. The Sheep reproached him for crying out, and said, "The master often lays hold of us, and we do not cry." "Yes," replied he, "but our case is not the same; for he catches you for the sake of your wool, but he lays hold of me for my very life!"

The Monkey Who Would
Be King

A Monkey once danced in an assembly of the Beasts, and so pleased them all by his performance that they elected him their King. A Fox, envying him the honor, discovered a piece of meat lying in a trap, and leading the Monkey to the place where it was said that she had found a store, and had not used it, but had kept it for him as treasure trove of his realm, and counselled him to lay hold of it. The Monkey approached carelessly, and was caught in the trap. On his accusing the Fox of purposely leading him into the snare, the Fox replied, "O Monkey, how can a creature with such a shallow mind as yours, ever hope to be King over the Beasts?"

The Bull and the Goat

A Bull pursued by a Lion, fled into a cave where a wild Goat had taken up his abode. At this intrusion, the Goat began molesting him and butting at him with his horns. "Don't suppose," said the Bull, "if I suffer this now, it is you I am afraid of. Let the Lion be once out of sight, and I will soon show you the difference between a Bull and a Goat."

Mean people take advantage of their neighbor's difficulties to annoy them, but the time will come when they will repent them of their insolence.

The Eagle
and the Jackdaw

An Eagle made a swoop from a high rock, and carried off a lamb. A Jackdaw, who saw the exploit, and thought that he could do the same, bore down with all the force he could muster upon a ram, intending to bear him off as a prize. But his claws became entangled in the wool, and he made such a fluttering in his efforts to escape, that the shepherd, seeing through the whole matter, came up and caught him. The shepherd, having clipped his wings, carried him home to his children at nightfall. "What bird is this, father, that you have brought us?" exclaimed the children. "Why," said he, "if you ask himself, he will tell you that he is an Eagle, but if you will take my word for it, I know him to be but a Jackdaw."

The Dog and the Oyster

A Dog, used to eating eggs, saw an Oyster, and opening his mouth to its widest extent, swallowed it down with the utmost relish, supposing it to be an egg. Soon afterwards suffering great pain in his stomach, he said, "I deserve all this torment, for my folly in thinking that everything round must be an egg."

Those who act without sufficient thought, will often fall into unsuspected danger.

The Ass and the Wolf

An Ass, feeding in a meadow, saw a Wolf approaching to seize him, and immediately pretended to be lame. The Wolf, coming up, inquired the cause of his lameness. The Ass said, that passing through a hedge he trod with his foot upon a sharp thorn, and requested the Wolf to pull it out, lest when he supped on him it should injure his throat. The Wolf, consenting, and lifting up his foot, gave his whole mind to the discovery of the thorn. As he did so, however, the Ass with his heels kicked the Wolf's teeth into his mouth, and galloped away. The Wolf, being thus fearfully mauled, said, "I am rightly served, for why did I attempt the art of healing, when my father only taught me the trade of a butcher?"

The Ass and the Frogs

An Ass carrying a load of wood, passed through a pond. As he was passing through the water, he lost his footing, and stumbled and fell, and not being able to rise on account of his load, he groaned heavily. Some Frogs frequenting the pool heard his lamentation, and said, "What would you do if you had to live here always as we do, when you make such a fuss about a mere fall into the water?"

Men often bear little grievances with less courage than they do large misfortunes.

The Two Wallets

Every man carries two Wallets, one before and one behind, and both full of faults. But the one before, is full of his neighbor's faults; the one behind, of his own. Thus it happens that men are blind to their own faults, but never lose sight of their neighbor's.

The Horse and the Loaded Ass

A Man who kept a Horse and an Ass was wont in his journeys to spare the Horse, and put all the burden upon the Ass's back. The Ass, who had been ailing for some time, besought the Horse one day to relieve him of part of his load. "For if," said he, "you would take a fair portion, I shall soon get well again. But if you refuse to help me, this weight will kill me." The Horse, however, bade the Ass get on, and not trouble him with his complaints. The Ass jogged on in silence, but presently, overcome with the weight of his burden, dropped down dead, as he had foretold. Upon this, the master coming up, unloosened the load from the dead Ass, and putting it upon the Horse's back, made him carry the Ass's carcass in addition. "Alas, for my ill nature!" said the Horse. "By refusing to bear my just portion of the load, I have now to carry the whole of it, with a dead weight into the bargain."

A disobliging temper carries its own punishment along with it.

The Hen
and the Swallow

A Hen finding the eggs of a viper, and carefully keeping them warm, nourished them into life. A Swallow, observing what she had done, said, "You silly creature! Why have you hatched these vipers, which, when they shall have grown, will inflict injury on all, beginning with yourself?"

The Shepherd Boy
and the Wolf

A Shepherd boy, who tended his flock not far from a village, used to amuse himself at times in crying out "Wolf! Wolf!" Twice or thrice his trick succeeded. The whole village came running out to his assistance, but all the return they got was to be laughed at for their pains. At last one day the Wolf came indeed. The Boy cried out in earnest, but his neighbors, supposing him to be at his old sport, paid no heed to his cries, and the Wolf devoured the Sheep. So the Boy learned, when it was too late, that liars are not believed even when they tell the truth.

The Crow and Mercury

A Crow caught in a snare prayed to Apollo to release him, making a vow to offer some frankincense at his shrine. On being rescued from his danger, however, he forgot his promise. Shortly afterwards, on being again caught in a second snare, as he passed by Apollo he made the same promise to offer frankincense to Mercury. Whereupon Mercury appeared, and said to him, "O thou most base fellow! how can I believe thee, who hast disowned and wronged thy former patron?"

Those who prove ungrateful to former benefactors, cannot hope for further aid.

The Crow and the Serpent

A Crow, in great want of food, saw a Serpent asleep in a sunny nook, and flying down, greedily seized him. The Serpent turning about, bit the Crow with a mortal wound. The Crow in the agony of death exclaimed: "O unhappy me! who have found in that which I deemed a happy windfall the source of my destruction."

There are many men who, like the Crow, endanger their lives, for the sake of finding treasure.

81

The Country Mouse
and the Town Mouse

Once upon a time, a Country Mouse who had a friend in town invited him, for old acquaintance sake, to pay him a visit in the country. The invitation being accepted in due form, the Country Mouse, though plain and rough and somewhat frugal in his nature, opened his heart and store, in honor of hospitality and an old friend. There was not a carefully stored-up morsel that he did not bring forth out of his larder: peas and barley, cheese parings, and nuts, hoping by quantity to make up what he feared was wanting in quality, and thus to suit the palate of his dainty guest. The Town Mouse, condescending to pick a bit here and a bit there, while the host sat nibbling a blade of barley-straw, at length exclaimed, "How is it, my good friend, that you can endure the dullness of this unpolished life? You are living like a toad in a hole. You can't really prefer these solitary rocks and woods to streets teeming with carriages and men. On my honor, you are wasting your time miserably here. We must make the most of life while it lasts. A mouse, you know, does not live forever. So come with me and I'll show you life and the town." Overpowered with

such fine words and so polished a manner, the Country Mouse assented, and they set out together on their journey to town. It was late in the evening when they crept stealthily into the city, and midnight ere they reached the great house where the Town Mouse took up his quarters. Here were couches of crimson velvet, carvings in ivory, and everything in short that denoted wealth and luxury. On the table were the remains of a splendid banquet, in preparation for which all the choicest shops in the town had been ransacked the day before. It was now the turn of the courtier to play the host. He placed his country friend on purple, ran to and fro to supply all his wants, pressed dish upon dish, and dainty upon dainty, and, as though he were waiting on a king, tasted every course ere he ventured to place it before his rustic cousin. The Country Mouse, for his part, affected to make himself quite at home, and blessed the good fortune that had wrought such a change in his way of life, when, in the midst of his enjoyment, as he thought with contempt of the poor fare he had left behind, the door flew open, and a party of revellers, returning from a late entertainment, burst into the room. The frightened friends jumped from the table in the greatest consternation and hid themselves in the first corner they could reach. No sooner did they venture to creep out again than the barking of dogs drove them back in still greater terror than before. At length, when things seemed quiet, the Country Mouse stole out from his hiding place, and bidding his friend good-bye, whispered in his ear, "Oh, my good sir, this fine mode of living may do for those who like it, but give me my barley bread in peace and security before the daintiest feast where Fear and Care are in waiting."

The Man and the Lion

Once upon a time a Man and a Lion were journeying together, and came at length to high words about which was the braver and stronger creature of the two. As the dispute became warmer they happened to pass by, on the roadside, a statue of a man strangling a lion. "See there," said the Man, "what more undeniable proof can you have of our superiority than that?" "That," said the Lion, "is your version of the story; let us be the sculptors, and for one lion under the feet of a man, you shall have twenty men under the paw of a lion."

Men are but sorry witnesses in their own cause.

The Farmer and the Dogs

A Farmer, during the winter, being shut up by the snow in his farmhouse, and sharply pressed for food, which he was unable to get about to procure, began consuming his own sheep. As the hard weather continued, he next ate up his goats. And at last—for there was no break in the weather—he betook himself to the oxen. Upon this, the Dogs said to one another, "Let us be off; for since the master, as we see, has had no pity on the oxen, how is it likely he will spare us?"

The Wind and the Sun

A dispute once arose between the Wind and the Sun, as to which was the stronger of the two, and they agreed to put the point upon this issue, that whichever made a traveller take off his cloak the soonest, should be accounted the more powerful. The Wind began, and blew with all his might and main a blast, cold and fierce as a Thracian storm, but the stronger he blew, the closer the traveller wrapped his cloak around him, and the tighter he grasped it with his hands. Then broke out the Sun, and with his welcome beams he dispersed the vapor and the cold. The traveller felt the genial warmth, and as the Sun shone brighter and brighter, he sat down, overcome with the heat, and cast his cloak on the ground.

Thus the Sun was declared the conqueror; and it has ever been deemed that persuasion is better than force, and that the sunshine of a kind and gentle manner will sooner lay open a poor man's heart than all the threatenings and force of blustering authority.

The Moon and Her Mother

The Moon once asked her Mother to make her a little cloak that would fit her well. "How," replied she, "can I make you a cloak to fit you, who are a New Moon, and then a Full Moon, and then again neither one nor the other?"

The Gnat and the Bull

A Gnat that had been buzzing about the head of a Bull, at length settling himself down upon his horn, begged the Bull's pardon for disturbing him. "But if," said he, "my weight at all inconveniences you, pray say so and I will be off in a moment." "Oh, never trouble your head about that," said the Bull, "for 'tis all one to me whether you go or stay, and, to say the truth, I did not know you were there."

The smaller the Mind the greater the Conceit.

The Thief
and the Innkeeper

A Thief hired a room in an inn, and stayed some days in the hope of stealing something which should enable him to pay his bill. When he had waited some days in vain, he saw the Innkeeper dressed in a new and handsome coat, and sitting before his door. The thief sat down beside him, and talked with him. As the conversation began to flag, the Thief yawned terribly, and at the same time howled like a Wolf. The Innkeeper said, "Why do you howl so fearfully?" "I will tell you," said the Thief, "but first let me ask you to hold my clothes, for I wish to leave them in your hands. I know not, sir, when I got this habit of yawning, or whether these attacks of howling were inflicted on me as a judgment for my crimes, or for any other cause, but this I do know, that when I yawn for the third time, I actually turn into a wolf, and attack men." With this speech he commenced a second fit of yawning, and again howled as a Wolf, as he had done at first. The Innkeeper, hearing his tale, and believing what he said, became greatly alarmed, and, rising from his seat, attempted to run away. The Thief laid hold of his coat, and entreated him to stop, saying, "Pray wait, sir, and hold my clothes, or I shall tear them to pieces in my fury, when I turn into a Wolf." At the same moment he yawned the third time, and set up a howl like a Wolf. The Innkeeper, frightened lest he should be attacked, left his new coat in the Thief's hand, and ran as fast as he could into the inn for safety. The Thief made off with his new coat, and did not return again to the inn.

It is often foolish to believe all that we are told.

The Sick Stag

A Stag that had fallen ill, lay down on the rich herbage of a lawn, close beside a wood, so that he might obtain an easy pasturage. But so many of the beasts came to see him—for he was a good sort of neighbor—that, one taking a little, and another a little, they soon ate up all the grass in the place. Thus, although recovered from his disease, he pined for want, and in the end lost both his substance and his life.

The Flea and the Man

A Man, very much annoyed with a Flea, caught him at last, and said, "Who are you who dare to feed on my limbs, and to cost me so much trouble in catching you?" The Flea replied, "O my dear sir, pray spare my life, and destroy me not, for I cannot possibly do you much harm." The Man, laughing, replied, "Now you shall certainly die by mine own hands, for no evil, whether it be small or large, ought to be tolerated."

The Farmer and His Sons

A Farmer being on the point of death, and wishing to show his sons the way to success in farming, called them to him and said, "My children, I am now departing from this life, but all I have to leave you, you will find in the vineyard." The sons, supposing that he referred to some hidden treasure, as soon as the old man died, set to work with their spades and ploughs and every implement that was at hand, and turned up the soil over and over again. They found, indeed, no treasure. But the vines, strengthened and improved by this thorough tillage, yielded a finer vintage than they had ever yielded before, and more than repaid the young husbandmen for all their trouble. So truly is industry in itself a treasure.

The Lion and the Fox

A Fox agreed to wait upon a Lion in the capacity of a servant. Each for a time performed the part belonging to his station: the Fox used to point out the prey, and the Lion fell upon it and seized it. But the Fox, beginning to think himself as good a beast as his master, begged to be allowed to hunt the game instead of finding it. His request was granted, but as he was in the act of making a descent upon a herd, the huntsman came out upon him, and he was himself made the prize.

Keep to your place, and your place will keep you.

The Shepherd
and the Wolf

A Shepherd once found the whelp of a Wolf, and brought it up, and after a while taught it to steal lambs from the neighboring flocks. The Wolf having shown himself an apt pupil, said to the Shepherd, "Since you have taught me to steal, you must keep a sharp lookout, or you will lose some of your own flock."

The Two Frogs
and the Well

Two Frogs dwelt in the same pool. The pool being dried up under the summer's heat, they left it, and set out together for another home. As they went along they chanced to pass a deep well, amply supplied with water, on seeing which, one of the Frogs said to the other, "Let us descend and make our abode in this well. It will furnish us with shelter and food." The other replied, with greater caution, "But suppose the water should fail us, how can we get out again from so great a depth?"

Do nothing without a regard to the consequence.

The Wolf and the Horse

As a Wolf was roaming over a farm, he came to a field of oats, but not being able to eat them, he left them and went his way. Presently meeting with a Horse, he bade him come with him into the field, "For," said he, "I have found some capital oats; and I have not tasted one, but have kept them all for you, for the very sound of your teeth is music to my ear." But the Horse replied: "A pretty fellow! If Wolves were able to eat oats, I suspect you would not have preferred your ears to your appetite."

Little thanks are due to him who only gives away what is of no use to himself.

The Kites and the Swans

The Kites of old time had, equally with the Swans, the privilege of song. But having heard the neigh of the horse, they were so enchanted with the sound, that they tried to imitate it, and, in trying to neigh, they forgot how to sing.

The desire for imaginary benefits often involves the loss of present blessings.

The Ass's Shadow

A Youth, one hot summer's day, hired an Ass to carry him from Athens to Megara. At midday the heat of the sun was so scorching, that he dismounted and would have sat down to repose himself under the shadow of the Ass. But the driver of the Ass disputed the place with him, declaring that he had an equal right to it with the other. "What!" said the

Youth, "did I not hire the Ass for the whole journey?" "Yes," said the other, "you hired the Ass, but not the Ass's shadow." While they were thus wrangling and fighting for the place, the Ass took to his heels and ran away.

In quarrelling over the shadow, we often lose the substance.

The Travellers
and the Plane Tree

Some Travellers, on a hot day in summer, oppressed with the noontide sun, perceiving a Plane tree near at hand, made straight for it and, throwing themselves on the ground, rested under its shade. Looking up, as they lay, towards the tree, they said one to another, "What a useless tree to man is this barren Plane!" But the Plane tree answered them, "Ungrateful creatures! At the very moment that you are enjoying benefit from me, you rail at me as being good for nothing."

The Bat and the Weasels

A Bat falling upon the ground was caught by a Weasel, of whom the Bat earnestly sought deliverance. The Weasel refused, saying that he was by nature the enemy of all birds. The Bat assured him that he was not a bird, but a mouse, and thus saved his life. Shortly afterwards the Bat again fell on the ground, and was caught by another Weasel, whom he likewise entreated not to eat him. The Weasel said that he had a special hostility to mice. The Bat assured him that he was not a mouse, but a bat; and thus a second time escaped.

It is wise to turn circumstances to good account.

The Fox and the Monkey

A Fox and a Monkey were travelling together on the same road. As they journeyed, they passed through a cemetery full of monuments. "All these monuments which you see," said the Monkey, "are erected in honor of my ancestors, who were in their day freed men, and citizens of great renown." The Fox replied, "You have chosen a most appropriate subject for your falsehoods, as I am sure none of your ancestors will be able to contradict you."

A false tale often betrays itself.

The Mouse and the Frog

A Mouse in an evil day made acquaintance with a Frog, and they set off on their travels together. The Frog, on pretense of great affection, and of keeping his companion out of harm's way, tied the Mouse's forefoot to his own hind leg, and thus they proceeded for some distance by land. Presently they came to some water, and the Frog, bidding the Mouse have good courage, began to swim across. They had scarcely, however, arrived midway, when the Frog took a sudden plunge to the bottom, dragging the unfortunate Mouse after him. But the struggling and floundering of the Mouse made so great a commotion in the water that it attracted the attention of a Kite, who, pouncing down, and bearing off the Mouse, carried away the Frog at the same time in his train.

Inconsiderate and ill-matched alliances generally end in ruin, and the man who compasses the destruction of his neighbor, is often caught in his own snare.

The Ass, the Cock, and the Lion

An Ass and a Cock lived in a farmyard together. One day a hungry Lion passing by, and seeing the Ass in good condition, resolved to make a meal of him. Now, they say that there is nothing a Lion hates so much as the crowing of a Cock, and at that moment the Cock happened to crow, and the Lion straightway made off with all haste from the spot. The Ass, mightily amused to think that a Lion should be frightened at a bird, plucked up courage and galloped after him, delighted with the notion of driving the King of Beasts before him. He had, however, gone no great distance, when the Lion turned sharply round upon him, and made an end of him in an instant.

Presumption begins in ignorance and ends in ruin.

The Wolf
in Sheep's Clothing

Once upon a time, a Wolf resolved to disguise himself, thinking that he should thus gain an easier livelihood. Having, therefore, clothed himself in a sheep's skin, he contrived to get in among a flock of Sheep, and feed along with them, so that even the Shepherd was deceived by the imposture. When night came on, and the fold was closed, the Wolf was shut up with the Sheep, and the door made fast. But the Shepherd, wanting something for his supper, and going in to fetch out a sheep, mistook the Wolf for one of them, and killed him on the spot.

The Lion, the Ass, and the Fox Go Hunting

The Lion, the Ass, and the Fox formed a party to go out hunting. They took a large booty, and when the sport was ended they decided to have a hearty meal. The Lion bade the Ass allot the spoil. So, dividing it into three equal parts, the Ass begged his friends to make their choice; at which the Lion, in great indignation, fell upon the Ass, and tore him to pieces. The Lion then bade the Fox make a division, who, gathering the whole into one great heap, reserved but the smallest mite for himself. "Ah! friend," said the Lion, "who taught you to make so equitable a division?" "I wanted no other lesson," replied the Fox, "than the Ass's fate."

The Cat and the Mice

A Cat, grown feeble with age, and no longer able to hunt the Mice as she was wont to do, bethought herself how she might entice them within reach of her paw. Thinking that she might pass herself off for a bag, or for a dead cat at least, she suspended herself by the hind legs from a peg, in the hope that the Mice would no longer be afraid to come near her. An old Mouse, who was wise enough to keep his distance, whispered to a friend, "Many a bag have I seen in my day, but never one with a cat's head." "Hang there, good Madam," said the other, "as long as you please, but I would not trust myself within reach of you though you were stuffed with straw."

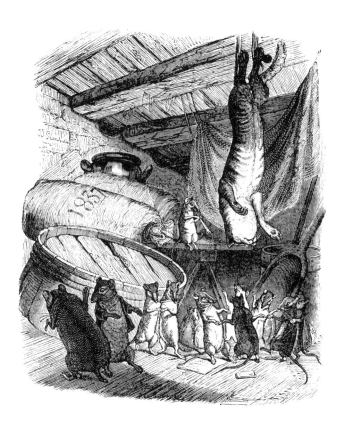

The Oaks and Jupiter

The Oaks presented a complaint to Jupiter, saying, "We bear for no purpose the burden of life, as of all the trees that grow we are the most continually in peril of the axe." Jupiter answered, "You have only to thank yourselves for the misfortunes to which you are exposed. For if you did not make such excellent pillars and posts, and prove yourselves so serviceable to the carpenters and the farmers, the axe would not so frequently be laid to your roots."

People often blame Providence for misfortunes for which their own natural dispositions are responsible.

The Nurse and the Wolf

A Wolf, roving about in search of food, passed by a door where a child was crying and its Nurse was chiding it. As he stood listening, he heard the Nurse say, "Now leave off crying this instant, or I'll throw you out to the Wolf." So, thinking that the old woman would be as good as her word, he waited quietly about the house, in expectation of a capital supper. But as it grew dark and the child became quiet, he again heard the Nurse, who was now fondling the child, say, "There's a good dear then; if the naughty Wolf comes for my child, we'll beat him to death, we will." The Wolf, disappointed and mortified, thought it was now high time to be going home, and, hungry as a wolf indeed, muttered as he went along: "This comes of heeding people who say one thing and mean another!"

The Wolf and the Sheep

A Wolf that had been bitten by a dog, and was in a very sad case, being unable to move, called to a Sheep, that was passing by, and begged her to fetch some water from the neighboring stream. "For if you," said he, "will bring me drink, I will find meat myself." "Yes," said the Sheep, "I have no doubt of it. For, if I come near enough to give you the drink, you will soon make mince-meat of *me*."

The Leopard and the Fox

A Leopard and a Fox had a contest as to which was the finer creature of the two. The Leopard put forward the beauty of its numberless spots; but the Fox replied, "It is better to have a versatile mind than a variegated body."

The Fox and the Woodsman

A Fox hard pressed by the hounds after a long run, came up to a man who was cutting wood, and begged him to afford some place where he might hide himself. The man showed him his own hut, and the Fox creeping in, hid himself in a corner. The Hunters presently came up, and asked the man whether he had seen the Fox. "No," said he, but pointed with his finger to the corner. They, however, not understanding the hint, were off again immediately. When the Fox perceived that they were out of sight, he began to steal off without saying a word. But the man upbraided him, saying, "Is this the way you take leave of your host, without a word of thanks for your safety?" "A pretty host!" said the Fox, turning round upon him. "If you had been as honest with your fingers as you were with your tongue, I should not have left your roof without bidding you farewell."

There is as much malice in a wink as in a word.

The Blind Man and the Whelp

A blind Man was accustomed to tell the species of any animal that was brought to him, by feeling over it with his hands. Once they brought to him a Wolf's whelp. He felt it all over, and being in doubt, said, "I know that I would not trust thee among a flock of sheep."

Evil dispositions are clearly shown.

The Sick Kite

A Kite, who had been long very ill, said to his mother, "Don't cry, mother, but go and pray to the gods that I may recover from this dreadful disease and pain." "Alas! child," said the mother, "which of the gods will listen to one who has robbed all their altars?"

A death-bed repentance is poor amends for the errors of a lifetime.

The Goatherd
and the Goats

It was a stormy day, and the snow was falling fast, when a Goatherd drove his Goats, all white with snow, into a deserted cave for shelter. There he found that a herd of Wild goats, more numerous and larger than his own, had already taken possession. So, thinking to secure them all, he left his own Goats to take care of themselves, and threw the branches which he had brought for them to the Wild goats to browse on. But, when the weather cleared up, he found his own Goats had perished from hunger, while the Wild goats were off and away to the hills and woods. So the Goatherd returned, a laughing-stock to his neighbors, having failed to gain the Wild goats, and having lost his own.

They who neglect their old friends for the sake of new, are rightly served if they lose both.

The Crab and the Fox

A Crab, forsaking the seashore, chose a neighboring green meadow as its feeding ground. A Fox came across him, and being very much famished ate him up. Just as he was on the point of being eaten, the Crab said, "I well deserve my fate; for what business had I on the land, when by my nature and habits I am only adapted for the sea?"

Contentment with our lot is an element of happiness.

The Lion in Love

It happened in days of old that a Lion fell in love with a Woodsman's daughter; and had the folly to ask her of her father in marriage. The Woodsman was not much pleased with the offer, and declined the honor of so dangerous an alliance. But upon the Lion threatening him with his royal displeasure, the poor man, seeing that so formidable a creature was not to be denied, hit at length upon this expedient: "I feel greatly flattered," said he, "with your proposal. But, noble sir, what great teeth you have got! And what great claws you have got! Where is the damsel that would not be frightened at such weapons as these? You must have your teeth drawn and your claws pared before you can be a suitable bridegroom for my daughter." The Lion straightway submitted, for what will not a body do for love? and then called upon the father to accept him as a son-in-law. But the Woodsman, no longer afraid of the tamed and disarmed bully, seized a stout cudgel and drove the unreasonable suitor from his door.

The Flies
and the Honey Pot

A Pot of Honey having been upset in a grocer's shop, the Flies came around it in swarms to eat it up. Nor would they move from the spot while there was a drop left. At length their feet became so clogged that they could not fly away, and, stifled in the luscious sweets, they exclaimed, "Miserable creatures that we are, who for the sake of an hour's pleasure have thrown away our lives!"

The Trumpeter
Taken Prisoner

A Trumpeter being taken prisoner in a battle, begged hard for quarter. "Spare me, good sirs, I beseech you," said he, "and put me not to death without cause, for I have killed no one myself, nor have I any arms but this trumpet only." "For that very reason," said they who had seized him, "shall you the sooner die. For without the spirit to fight, yourself, you stir up others to warfare and bloodshed."

He who invites to strife is worse than he who takes part in it.

The Peasant
and the Apple Tree

A Peasant had in his garden an Apple tree which bore no fruit, but only served as a harbor for the sparrows and grasshoppers. He resolved to cut it down, and, taking his axe in his hand, made a bold stroke at its roots. The grasshoppers and sparrows entreated him not to cut down the tree that sheltered them, but to spare it, and they would sing to him and lighten his labors. He paid no attention to their request, but gave the tree a second and a third blow with his axe. When he reached the hollow of the tree, he found a hive full of honey. Having tasted the honeycomb, he threw down his axe, and, looking on the tree as sacred, took great care of it.

Self interest alone moves some men.

The Falconer
and the Partridge

A Falconer having taken a Partridge in his net, the bird cried out sorrowfully, "Let me go, good Master Falconer, and I promise I will decoy other Partridges into your net." "No," said the man, "whatever I might have done, I am determined now not to spare you; for there is no death too bad for him who is ready to betray his friends."

The Wise
and the Foolish Frogs

Two Frogs were neighbors. One inhabited a deep pond, far removed from public view; the other lived in a gully containing little water, and traversed by a country road. He that lived in the pond warned his friend, and entreated him to change his residence, and to come and live with him, saying that he would enjoy greater safety from danger and more abundant food. The other refused, saying that he felt it so very hard to remove from a place to which he had become accustomed. A few days afterwards, a heavy wagon passed through the gully, and crushed him to death under its wheels.

A wilful man will have his own way to his own hurt.

The Wild Boar and the Fox

A wild Boar was whetting his tusks against a tree, when a Fox coming by asked why he did so. "For," said he, "I see no reason for it; there is neither hunter nor hound in sight, nor any other danger, that I can see, at hand." "True," replied the Boar, "but when that danger does arise, I shall have something else to do than to sharpen my weapons."

It is too late to whet the sword once the trumpet sounds to draw it.

The Dogs and the Fox

Some Dogs, finding the skin of a lion, began to tear
it in pieces with their teeth. A Fox, seeing them, said,
"If this lion were alive, you would soon find out that
his claws were stronger than your teeth."

It is easy to kick a man that is down.

The Wolves
and the Sheep Dogs

The Wolves thus addressed the Sheep Dogs: "Why
should you, who are like us in so many things, not
be entirely of one mind with us, and live with us as
brothers should? We differ from you in one point
only: we live in freedom, but you bow down to, and
slave for, men; who, in return for your services, flog
you with whips, and put collars on your necks.

They make you also guard their sheep, and while they eat the mutton, they throw only the bones to you. If you will be persuaded by us, you will give us the sheep, and we will enjoy them in common, till we all are surfeited." The Dogs listened favorably to these proposals, and, entering the den of the Wolves, they were set upon and torn to pieces.

The Lion, the Mouse, and the Fox

A Lion, fatigued by the heat of a summer's day, fell fast asleep in his den. A Mouse ran over his mane and ears, and woke him from his slumbers. He rose up and shook himself in great wrath, and searched every corner of his den to find the Mouse. A Fox, seeing him, said: "A fine Lion you are, to be frightened of a Mouse." "'Tis not the Mouse I fear," said the Lion; "I resent his familiarity and ill-breeding."

Little liberties are great offenses.

119

The Wolf and the Crane

A Wolf had got a bone stuck in his throat, and in the greatest agony ran up and down, beseeching every animal he met to relieve him, while at the same time hinting at a very handsome reward to the successful operator. A Crane, moved by his entreaties and promises, ventured her long neck down the Wolf's throat, and drew out the bone. She then modestly asked for the promised reward. To which, the Wolf, grinning and showing his teeth, replied with seeming indignation, "Ungrateful creature! to ask for any other reward than that you have put your head into a Wolf's jaws, and brought it safe out again!"

Those who are charitable only in the hope of a return, must not be surprised if, in their dealings with evil men, they meet with more jeers than thanks.

The Prophet

A Wizard sitting in the marketplace, told the fortunes of the passersby. A person ran up in great haste, and announced to him that the doors of his house had been broken open, and that all his goods were being stolen. He sighed heavily, and hastened away as fast as he could run. A neighbor saw him running, and said, "Oh! you fellow there! you say you can foretell the fortunes of others; how is it you did not foresee your own?"

The War Horse
and the Miller

A War Horse, feeling the infirmities of age, betook himself to a mill instead of going out to battle. But when he was compelled to grind instead of serving in the wars, he bewailed his change of fortune, and called to mind his former state, saying, "Ah! Miller, I had intended to go campaigning before, but I was barbed from counter to tail, and a man went along to groom me; and now, I cannot tell what made me to prefer the mill to the battle." "Stop," said the Miller, "harping on what used to be. For it is the common lot of mortals to sustain the ups and downs of fortune."

The Traveller and Fortune

A Traveller, wearied with a long journey, lay down overcome with fatigue on the very brink of a deep well. Being within an inch of falling into the water, Dame Fortune, it is said, appeared to him, and waking him from his slumber, thus addressed him: "Good Sir, pray wake up: for should you fall into the well, the blame will be thrown on me, and I shall get an ill name among mortals. For I find that men are sure to impute their calamities to me, however much their own folly may have brought them on themselves."

Everyone is more or less master of his own fate.

The Dog in the Manger

A Dog made his bed in a Manger, and lay snarling and growling to keep the horses from their provender. "See," said one of them, "what a miserable cur, who neither can eat corn himself, nor will allow those to eat it who can!"

The Horse and His Rider

A Horse soldier took the utmost pains with his charger. As long as the war lasted, he looked upon him as his fellow helper in all emergencies, and fed him carefully with hay and corn. When the war was over, he only allowed him chaff to eat, and made him carry heavy loads of wood, and subjected him to much slavish drudgery and ill-treatment. War, however, being again proclaimed, and the trumpet summoning him to his standard, the Soldier put on his charger its military trappings, and mounted, being clad in his heavy coat of mail. The Horse fell down straightway under the weight, no longer equal to the burden, and said to his master, "You must now go to the war on foot, for you have transformed me from a Horse into an Ass. How can you expect that I can again turn in a moment from an Ass to a Horse?"

The Farmer and the Lion

A Lion entered one day into a farmyard, and the Farmer, wishing to catch him, shut the gate. When the Lion found that he could not get out, he began at once to attack the sheep, and then betook himself to the oxen. So the Farmer, afraid for himself, now opened the gate, and the Lion made off as fast as he could. The Farmer's wife, who had observed it all, when she saw her husband in great trouble at the loss of his cattle, cried out: "You are rightly served; for what could have made you so mad as to wish to obtain a creature, whom, if you saw at a distance, you would wish further off."

Better scare a thief than snare him.

The Fir Tree
and the Bramble

A Fir tree was once boasting of itself to a Bramble. "You are of no use at all; but how could barns and houses be built without me?" "Good sir," said the Bramble, "when the woodsmen come here with their axes and saws, what would you give to be a Bramble and not a Fir?"

A humble lot in security is better than the dangers that encompass the high and the haughty.

The Husbandman
and the Stork

A Husbandman fixed a net in his field to catch the Cranes that came to feed on his new-sown corn. When he went to examine the net, and see what Cranes he had taken, a Stork was found among the number. "Spare me," cried the Stork, "and let me go. I am no Crane. I have eaten none of your corn. I am a poor innocent Stork, as you may see—the most pious and dutiful of birds. I honor and succor my father and mother. I—" But the Husbandman cut him short. "All this may be true enough, I dare say, but this I know, that I have caught you with those who were destroying my crops, and you must suffer with the company in which you are taken."

Ill company proves more than fair possessions.

The Monkey and the Camel

At a great meeting of the Beasts, the Monkey stood up to dance. Having greatly distinguished himself, and being applauded by all present, it roused the envy of the Camel, who came forward and began to dance also. But the Camel made himself so utterly absurd, that all the Beasts in indignation set upon him with clubs and drove him out of the ring.

It is foolish vanity to try to ape our betters.

The Monkey
and the Dolphin

It was an old custom among sailors to carry about with them little Maltese lapdogs, or Monkeys, to amuse them on the voyage. So it happened once upon a time that a man took with him a Monkey as a companion on board ship. While they were off Sunium, the famous promontory of Attica, the ship was caught in a violent storm and, being capsized, all on board were thrown in the water, and had to swim for land as best they could. And among them was the Monkey. A Dolphin saw him struggling, and, taking him for a man, went to his assistance and bore him on his back straight for shore. When they had just got opposite Piraeus, the harbor of Athens, the Dolphin asked the Monkey if he was an Athenian. "Yes," answered the Monkey, assuredly, "and of one of the first families in the place." "Then of course, you know Piraeus," said the Dolphin. "Oh, yes," said the Monkey, who thought it was the name of some distinguished citizen, "He is one of my most intimate friends." Indignant at so gross a deceit and falsehood, the Dolphin dived to the bottom and left the lying Monkey to his fate.

The Hares and the Lions

The Hares harangued the assembly and argued that all should be on an equality. The Lions made this reply: "Your words, O Hares! are good, but they lack both claws and teeth such as we have."

The Lion and the Bull

A Lion, greatly desirous to capture a Bull, and yet afraid to attack him on account of his great size, resorted to a trick to insure his destruction. He approached him and said, "I have slain a fine sheep, my friend, and if you will come home and partake of him with me, I shall be delighted to have your company." The Lion said this in the hope that, as the Bull was in the act of reclining to eat, he might attack him to advantage, and make his meal on him. The Bull, however, on his approach to his den, saw the huge spits and giant cauldrons, and no sign whatever of the sheep, and, without saying a word, quietly took his departure. The Lion inquired why he went off so abruptly without a word of salutation to his host, who had not given him any cause of offense. "I have reasons enough," said the Bull. "I see no indication whatever of your having slaughtered a sheep, while I do see, very plainly, every preparation for your dining on a Bull."

The Thieves and the Cock

Some Thieves broke into a house, and found nothing but a Cock, whom they stole, and got off as fast as they could. On arriving at home they proceeded to kill the Cock, who thus pleaded for his life: "Pray spare me. I am very serviceable to men. I wake them up in the night to their work." "That is the very reason why we must the more kill you," replied the Thieves, "for when you wake your neighbors, you entirely put an end to our business."

The safeguards of virtue are hateful to those disposed to evil.

The Ass and His Driver

An Ass that was being driven along the road by his Master, started on ahead, and, leaving the beaten track, made as fast as he could for the edge of a precipice. When he was just on the point of falling over, his Master ran up, and, seizing him by the tail, endeavored to pull him back. But the Ass resisted and pulled the contrary way, and the man let go his hold, saying, "Well, Jack, if you will be Master, I cannot help it. A wilful beast must go his own way."

The Hares and the Frogs

Once upon a time the Hares, driven desperate by the many enemies that compassed them about on every side, came to the sad resolution that there was nothing left for them but to make away with themselves, one and all. Off they scuttled to a lake hard by, determined to drown themselves as the most miserable of creatures. A shoal of Frogs seated upon the bank, frightened at the approach of the Hares, leaped in the greatest alarm and confusion into the water. "Nay, then, my friends," said the Hare that was foremost, "our case is not so desperate yet; for here are other poor creatures more faint-hearted than ourselves."

Take not comfort, but courage, from another's distress, and be sure, whatever your misery, that there are some whose lot you would not exchange with your own.

The Lion and the Hare

A Lion came across a Hare, who was fast asleep on the forest floor. He was just in the act of seizing her, when a fine young Hart trotted by, and he left the Hare to follow him. The Hare, scared by the noise, awoke, and scuttled away. The Lion was not able after a long chase to catch the Hart, and returned to feed upon the Hare. On finding that the Hare also had run off, he said, "I am rightly served, for having let go the food that I had in my hand for the chance of obtaining more."

The Man
Bitten by a Dog

A Man who had been bitten by a Dog, was going about asking who would cure him. One that met him said, "Sir, if you would be cured, take a bit of bread and dip it in the blood of the wound, and give it to the dog that bit you." The Man smiled, and said, "If I were to follow your advice, I should be bitten by all the dogs in the city."

He who proclaims himself ready to buy up his enemies will never want a supply of them.

The Two Dogs

A Man had two dogs: a Hound, trained to assist him in his sports, and a House dog, taught to watch the house. When he returned home after a good day's sport, he always gave the House dog a large share of his spoil. The Hound, feeling much aggrieved at this, reproached his companion, saying, "It is very hard to have all this labor, while you, who do not assist in the chase, luxuriate on the fruits of my exertions." The House dog replied, "Do not blame me, my friend, but find fault with the master, who has not taught me to labor, but to depend for subsistence on the labor of others."

Children are not to be blamed for the faults of their parents.

The Flea and the Ox

A Flea thus questioned the Ox: "What ails you, that, being so huge and strong, you submit to the wrongs you receive from men, and thus slave for them day by day, while I, being so small a creature, mercilessly feed on their flesh, and drink their blood without stint?" The Ox replied: "I do not wish to be ungrateful, for I am loved and well cared for by men and they often pat my head and shoulders." "Woe's me!" said the Flea; "this very patting which you like, whenever it happens to me, brings with it my inevitable destruction."

The Boy Bathing

A Boy was bathing in a river, and, getting out of his depth, was on the point of sinking when he saw a wayfarer coming by, to whom he called out for help with all his might and main. The Man began to read the Boy a lecture for his foolhardiness, but the Boy cried out, "O, save me now, sir! and read me the lecture afterwards."

The Ass
and the Grasshoppers

An Ass, hearing some Grasshoppers chirping, was delighted with the music, and determining, if he could, to rival them, asked them what it was they fed upon to make them sing so sweetly? When they told him that they supped upon nothing but dew, the Ass betook himself to the same diet, and soon died of hunger.

One man's meat is another man's poison.

The Peacock
and the Crane

A Peacock, spreading its gorgeous tail, mocked a Crane that passed by, ridiculing the ashen hue of its plumage, and saying, "I am robed, like a king, in gold and purple, and all the colors of the rainbow, while you have not a bit of color on your wings."

"True," replied the Crane, "but I soar to the heights of heaven, and lift up my voice to the stars, while you walk below, like a cock, among the birds of the barnyard."

Fine feathers do not make fine birds.

The Shepherd and the Sea

A Shepherd moved down his flock to feed near the shore, and beholding the Sea lying in a smooth and breathless calm, he was seized with a strong desire to sail over it. So he sold all his sheep and bought a cargo of dates, and loaded a vessel, and set sail. He had not gone far when a storm arose; his ship was wrecked, and his dates and everything lost, and he himself with difficulty escaped to land. Not long after, when the Sea was again calm, and one of his friends came up to him and was admiring its calm, he said, "Have a care, my good fellow, of that smooth surface. It is only looking out for your dates."

The Ass
in the Lion's Skin

An Ass, having put on a Lion's skin, roamed about frightening all the silly animals he met with. Seeing a Fox, he tried to alarm him also. But the Fox, having heard his voice, said, "Well, to be sure! And I should have been frightened too, if I had not heard you bray."

The Gnat and the Lion

A Gnat came and said to a Lion, "I do not the least fear you, nor are you stronger than I am. For in what does your strength consist? You can scratch with your claws, and bite with your teeth—so can a woman in her quarrels. I repeat that I am altogether more powerful than you, and if you doubt it, let us fight and see who will conquer." The Gnat, having sounded his horn, fastened itself upon the Lion, and stung him on the nostrils and the parts of the face devoid of hair. The Lion, trying to crush him, tore himself with his claws, until he punished himself severely. The Gnat thus prevailed over the Lion, and, buzzing about in a song of triumph, flew away. But shortly afterwards he became entangled in the meshes of a cobweb, and was eaten by a spider. He greatly lamented his fate, saying, "Woe is me! That I, who can wage war successfully with the hugest beasts, should perish myself from an insignificant spider!"

The Brazier and His Dog

There was a certain Brazier who had a little Dog. While he hammered away at his metal, the Dog slept, but whenever he sat down to his dinner the Dog woke up. "Sluggard cur!" said the Brazier, throwing him a bone. "You sleep through the noise of the anvil, but wake up at the first clatter of my teeth."

Men are awake enough to their own interests, who turn a deaf ear to their friend's distress.

The Goose
with the Golden Eggs

A certain man had the good fortune to possess a Goose that laid him a Golden Egg every day. But dissatisfied with so slow an income, and thinking to seize the whole treasure at once, he killed the Goose, and, cutting her open, found her—just what any other goose would be!

Much wants more and loses all.

The Man and the Satyr

A Man and a Satyr having struck up an acquaintance sat down together to eat. The day being wintry and cold, the Man put his fingers to his mouth and blew upon them. "What's that for, my friend?" asked the Satyr. "My hands are so cold," said the Man, "I do it to warm them." In a little while some hot food was placed before them, and the Man, raising the dish to his mouth, again blew upon it. "And what's the meaning of that, now?" said the Satyr. "Oh," replied the Man, "my porridge is so hot, I do it to cool it." "Nay, then," said the Satyr, "from this moment I renounce your friendship, for I will have nothing to do with one who blows hot and cold with the same mouth."

The Spendthrift and the Swallow

A young man, a great spendthrift, had run through all his patrimony, and had but one good cloak left. He happened to see a Swallow, which had appeared before its season, skimming along a pool and twittering gaily. He supposed that summer had come, and went and sold his cloak. Not many days after, the winter having set in again with renewed frost and cold, he found the unfortunate Swallow lifeless on the ground, and said, "Unhappy bird! what have you done? By thus appearing before the springtime you have not only killed yourself, but you have wrought my destruction also."

The Fox and the Stork

A Fox one day invited a Stork to dinner, and being disposed to divert himself at the expense of his guest, provided nothing for the entertainment but some thin soup in a shallow dish. This the Fox lapped up very readily, while the Stork, unable to gain a mouthful with her long narrow bill, was as hungry at the end of dinner as when she began. The Fox meanwhile professed his regret at seeing her eat so sparingly, and feared that the dish was not seasoned to her mind. The Stork said little, but begged that the Fox would do her the honor of returning her visit, and accordingly he agreed to dine with her on the following day. He arrived true to his appointment, and the dinner was ordered forthwith. But when it was served up, he found to his dismay that it was contained in a narrow-necked vessel, down which the Stork readily thrust her long neck and bill, while he was obliged to content himself with licking the neck of the jar. Unable to satisfy his hunger, he retired with as good a grace as he could, observing that he could hardly find fault with his entertainer, who had only paid him back in his own coin.

144

The Walnut Tree

A Walnut tree standing by the roadside bore an abundant crop of fruit. The passersby broke its branches with stones and sticks for the sake of the nuts. The Walnut tree pitiously exclaimed, "O wretched me! that those whom I cheer with my fruit should repay me with these painful requitals!"

There are many thoughtless people, who return only evil for good.

The Belly and the Members

In former days, when all a man's limbs did not work together as amicably as they do now, but each had a will and a way of its own, the Members generally began to find fault with the Belly for spending an idle, luxurious life, while they were wholly occupied in laboring for its support, and ministering to its wants and pleasures. So they entered into a conspiracy to cut off its supplies for the future. The Hands were no longer to carry food to the Mouth, nor the Mouth to receive the food, nor the Teeth to chew it. They had not long persisted in this course of starving the Belly into subjection, ere they all began, one by one, to fail and flag, and the whole body to pine away. Then the Members were convinced that the Belly also, cumbersome and useless as it seemed, had an important function of its own, and that they could no more do without it than it could do without them, and that if they would have the constitution of the body in a healthy state, they must work together, each in his proper sphere, for the common good of all.

The Widow and the Hen

A Widow kept a Hen that laid an egg every morning. Thought the woman to herself, "If I double my Hen's allowance of barley, she will lay twice a day." So she tried her plan, and the Hen became so fat and sleek, that she left off laying at all.

The Lioness

There was a great stir among all the Beasts, as to which could boast of the largest family. So they came to the Lioness. "And how many," said they, "do you have at a birth?" "One," said she, grimly, "but that one is a Lion."

Quality comes before quantity.

Mercury
and the Woodsman

A Woodsman was felling a tree on the bank of a river, and by chance let slip his axe into the water, where it immediately sank to the bottom. Being thereupon in great distress, he sat down by the side of the stream and lamented his loss bitterly. But Mercury, whose river it was, taking compassion on him, appeared at the instant before him, and hearing from him the cause of his sorrow, dived to the bottom of the river. Bringing up a golden axe, he asked the Woodsman if that were his. Upon the man's denying it, Mercury dived a second time, and brought up one of silver. Again the man denied that it was his. So, diving a third time, he produced the identical axe which the man had lost. "That is mine!" said the Woodsman, delighted to have recovered his own. So pleased was Mercury with the fellow's truth and honesty, that he at once made him a present of the other two.

The man went to his companions, and giving them an account of what had happened to him, one of them determined to try whether he might not have the like good fortune. So, repairing to the same place, as if for the purpose of cutting wood, he let slip his axe on purpose into the river, and then sat down on the bank, and made a great show of weeping. Mercury appeared as before, and hearing from him that his tears were caused by the loss of his axe, dived once more into the stream, and bringing up a golden axe, asked him if that was the axe he had lost. "Aye, surely," said the man, eagerly, and he was about to grasp the treasure, when Mercury, to punish his impudence and lying, not only refused to give him that, but would not so much as restore him his own axe again.

Honesty is the best policy.

The Geese and the Cranes

Some Geese and some Cranes fed together in the same field. One day the sportsmen came suddenly down upon them. The Cranes, being light of body, flew off in a moment and escaped, but the Geese, weighed down by their fat, were all taken.

In bad times, they fare best who have least to fetter them.

The Jackdaw and the Doves

A Jackdaw, seeing some Doves in a cote abundantly provided with food, painted himself white, and joined himself to them, so that he might enjoy a share of their good living. The Doves, as long as he was silent, supposing him to be one of themselves, admitted him to their cote. But when, forgetting himself one day, he began to chatter, they discovered his true character, and drove him forth, pecking him with their beaks. Failing to obtain food among the Doves, he betook himself again to the Jackdaws, but they too, not recognizing him on account of his changed color, expelled him from living with them. So, desiring two objects, he obtained neither.

The Wasps, the Partridges, and the Farmer

The Wasps and the Partridges, overcome with thirst, came to a Farmer and besought him to give them some water to drink. They promised amply to repay him the favor which they asked. The Partridges declared that they would dig around his vines, and make them produce finer grapes. The Wasps said that they would keep guard, and drive off thieves with their stings. The Farmer, interrupting them, said: "I have already two oxen, who, without making any promises, do all these things. It is surely better for me to give the water to them than to you."

The Ass and His Masters

An Ass that belonged to a Gardener, and had little to eat and much to do, besought Jupiter to release him from the Gardener's service, and give him another master. Jupiter, angry at his discontent, made him over to a Potter. He had now heavier burdens to carry than before, and again appealed to Jupiter to relieve him, who accordingly contrived that he should be sold to a Tanner. The Ass having now fallen into worse hands than ever, and daily observing how his master was employed, exclaimed with a groan, "Alas, wretch that I am! It had been better for me to have remained content with my former masters, for now I see that my present owner not only works me harder while living, but will not even spare my hide when I am dead!"

He that is discontented in one place will seldom be happy in another.

The Astronomer

An Astronomer used to walk out every night to gaze upon the stars. It happened one night, that, as he was wandering in the outskirts of the city with his whole thoughts rapt up in the skies, he fell into a well. On his holloaing and calling out, one who heard his cries ran up to him, and when he had listened to his story, said, "My good man, while you are trying to pry into the mysteries of heaven, you ought not overlook the common objects that are under your feet."

The Charger and the Ass

A Charger adorned with his fine trappings came thundering along the road, exciting the envy of a poor Ass who was trudging along the same way with a heavy load upon his back. "Get out of my road!" said the proud Charger, "or I shall trample you under my feet." The Ass said nothing, but quickly moved to one side to let the horse pass. Not long afterwards the Charger was engaged in the wars, and being badly wounded in battle was rendered unfit for military service, and sent to work upon a farm. When the Ass saw him dragging with great labor a heavy wagon, he understood how little reason he had had to envy one who, by his overbearing spirit in the time of his prosperity, had lost those friends who might have succored him in time of need.

The Pomegranate, the Apple, and the Bramble

The Pomegranate and the Apple had a contest on the score of beauty. When words ran high and the strife waxed dangerous, a Bramble, thrusting his head from a neighboring bush, cried out, "We have disputed long enough; let there be no more rivalry betwixt the two of us."

The most insignificant creatures are generally the most presuming.

The Mole
and Her Mother

Said a young Mole to her Mother, "Mother, I can see." So, in order to try her, her Mother put a lump of frankincense before her, and asked her what it was. "A stone," said the young one. "O, my child!" said the Mother, "not only do you not see, but you cannot even smell."

Brag upon one defect, and betray another.

The Fox without a Tail

A Fox being caught in a trap, was glad to save his neck by leaving his tail behind him. But upon coming abroad into the world, he began to be so sensible of the disgrace such a defect would bring upon him, that he almost wished he had died rather than come away without it. However, resolving to make the best of a bad matter, he called a meeting of the rest of the Foxes, and proposed that all should follow his example. "You have no notion," said he, "of the ease and comfort with which I now move about: I could never have believed it if I had not tried it myself; but really, when one comes to reason upon it, a tail is such an ugly, inconvenient, unnecessary appendage, that the only wonder is that, as Foxes, we could have put up with it so long. I propose, therefore, my worthy brethren, that you all profit by the experience that I am most willing to afford you, and that all Foxes from this day forward cut off their tails." Upon this one of the oldest stepped forward, and said, "I rather think, my friend, that you would not have advised us to part with our tails, if there were any chance of recovering your own."

The Bear and the Fox

A Bear used to boast of his excessive love for Man, saying that he never worried or mauled him when dead. The Fox observed, with a smile, "I shouldn't so much care what you did to Man after he was dead, if you never ate him alive."

157

The Murderer

A Man committed a murder, and was pursued by the relations of the man whom he murdered. On his reaching the river Nile he saw a lion on its bank, and being fearfully afraid, he climbed up a tree. He found a serpent in the upper branches of the tree, and again being greatly alarmed he threw himself into the river, where a crocodile caught him and ate him. Thus the earth, the air, and the water, alike refused shelter to a Murderer.

The Tortoise and the Eagle

A Tortoise, dissatisfied with his lowly life when he beheld so many of the birds, his neighbors, disporting themselves in the clouds, and thinking that, if he could but once get up into the air, he could soar with the best of them, called one day upon an Eagle and offered him all the treasures of the Ocean if he could only teach him to fly. The Eagle would have declined the task, assuring him that the thing was not only absurd but impossible, but being further pressed by the entreaties and promises of the Tortoise, he at length consented to do for him the best he could. So he took him up to a great height and loosed his hold upon him. "Now, then!" cried the Eagle; but the Tortoise, before he could answer him a word, fell plump upon a rock, and was dashed to pieces.

Pride shall have a fall.

The Great
and the Little Fishes

A Fisherman was drawing up a net which he had cast into the sea, and which was full of all sorts of fish. The Little Fish escaped through the meshes of the net, and got back into the deep, but the Great Fish were all caught and hauled into the ship.

Our insignificance is often the cause of our safety.

The Marriage of the Sun

Once upon a time, during a very warm summer, it was widely reported that the Sun was going to be married. All the birds and beasts were delighted at the thought, and the Frogs, above all others, were determined to have a good holiday. But an old Toad put a stop to their festivities by observing that it was an occasion for sorrow rather than joy. "For if," said he, "the Sun of himself now parches up the marshes so that we can hardly bear it, what will become of us if he should have a dozen little Suns in addition?"

The Old Woman
and Her Maids

A thrifty old Widow kept two Servant maids, whom she used to call up to their work at cock-crow. The Maids disliked exceedingly this early rising, and determined between themselves to wring off the Cock's neck, as he was the cause of all their trouble by waking their mistress so early. They had no sooner done this, than the old lady missing her usual alarm, and afraid of oversleeping herself, continually mistook the time of day, and roused them up at midnight.

Too much cunning overreaches itself.

Venus and the Cat

A Cat having fallen in love with a young man, besought Venus to change her into a girl, in the hope of gaining his affections. The Goddess, taking compassion on her weakness, metamorphosed her into a fair damsel, and the young man, enamored of her beauty, led her home as his bride. As they were sitting in their chamber, Venus, wishing to know whether in changing her form she had also changed her nature, set down a Mouse before her. The Girl, forgetful of her new condition, started from her seat, and pounced upon the Mouse as if she would have eaten it on the spot. Whereupon the Goddess, provoked at her frivolity, straightway turned her into a Cat again.

What is bred in the bone, will never out of the flesh.

The Fishermen

Some Fishermen were out trawling their nets. Perceiving them to be very heavy, they danced about for joy, and supposed that they had taken a large catch of fish. When they had dragged the nets to the shore they found but few fish, and that the nets were full of sand and stones, and they were beyond measure cast down—not so much at the disappointment which had befallen them, as because they had formed such very different expectations. One of their company, an old man, said, "Let us cease lamenting, my mates, for, as it seems to me, sorrow is always the twin sister of joy, and it was only to be looked for that we, who just now were over-rejoiced, should next have something to make us sad."

Storms often gather from a clear sky.

The Brother and the Sister

A Father had one son and one daughter; the former remarkable for his good looks; the latter for her extraordinary ugliness. While they were playing one day, they happened by chance to look together into a mirror which was placed on their mother's chair. The Brother congratulated himself on his good looks, while his Sister grew angry, unable to bear the self-praise of her Brother. Hearing everything he said as a reflection upon herself, she ran off to her Father to be revenged upon her unkind Brother. The Father embraced them both and said, "I wish you both every day to look into the mirror: you, my son, that you may not spoil your handsomeness by evil conduct, and you, my daughter, that you may make up for your want of beauty by your virtues."

The Mischievous Dog

There was a Dog so wild and mischievous, that his master was obliged to fasten a heavy clog about his neck, to prevent him biting and worrying his neighbors. The Dog, priding himself upon his badge, paraded in the marketplace, shaking his clog to attract attention. But a sly friend whispered to him, "The less noise you make, the better. Your mark of distinction is no reward of merit, but a badge of disgrace!"

Men often mistake notoriety for fame, and would rather be remarked for their vices or follies, than not to be noticed at all.

The Hen and the Cat

A Cat, hearing that a Hen was laid up sick in her nest, paid her a visit of condolence, and creeping up to her said, "How are you, my dear friend? What can I do for you? What are you in want of? Only tell me, if there is anything in the world that I can bring you to keep up your spirits, and don't be alarmed." "Thank you," said the Hen, "but if you would be good enough to leave me, I have no fear but I shall soon be well."

Unbidden guests are often welcomest when they are gone.

The Dog, the Cock, and the Fox

A Dog and a Cock, having struck up an acquaintance, went out on their travels together. Nightfall found them in a forest, so the Cock, flying up on a tree, perched among the branches, while the Dog dozed below at the foot. As the night passed away and the day dawned, the Cock, according to his custom, set up a shrill crowing. A Fox hearing him, and thinking to make a meal of him, came and stood under the tree, and thus addressed him: "Thou art a good little bird, and most useful to thy fellow-creatures. Come down, then, that we may sing our matins and rejoice together." The Cock replied, "Go, my good friend, to the foot of the tree, and call the sacristan to toll the bell." But as the Fox went to call him, the Dog jumped out in a moment, and seized the Fox and made an end of him.

The Boy
and the Scorpion

A Boy was hunting Locusts upon a wall and had caught a great number of them, when, seeing a Scorpion, he mistook it for another Locust, and was hollowing his hand to catch it, when the Scorpion, lifting up his sting, said: "I wish you had done it, for I would soon have made you drop me, and the Locusts into the bargain."

The Viper and the File

A Viper, entering into a smith's shop, began looking about for something to eat. At length, seeing a File, he went up to it and commenced biting at it. But the File bade him leave him alone, saying, "You are likely to get little from me, whose business it is to bite others."

The Rich Man
and the Tanner

A Rich Man lived near a Tanner, and not being able to bear the unpleasant smell of the tanning yard, he pressed his neighbor to go away. The Tanner put off his departure from time to time, saying that he would remove soon. But as he still continued to stay, it came to pass, as time went on, that the Rich Man became accustomed to the smell, and feeling no manner of inconvenience, made no further complaints.

The Bowman
and the Lion

A Man who was very skilful with his bow, went up into the mountains to hunt. At his approach there was instantly a great consternation and rout among all the wild beasts, the Lion alone showing any determination to fight. "Stop," said the Bowman to him, "and await my messenger, who has something to say to you." With that he sent an arrow after the Lion, and wounded him in the side. The Lion, smarting with anguish, fled into the depth of the thickets, but a Fox, seeing him run, bade him take courage, and face his enemy. "No," said the Lion, "you will not persuade me to that; for if the messenger he sends is so sharp, what must be the power of him who sends it?"

The Fox and the Bramble

A Fox, mounting a hedge, when he was about to fall caught hold of a bramble. Having pricked and grievously torn the soles of his feet, he accused the Bramble, because, when he had fled to her for assistance, she had used him worse than the hedge itself. The Bramble, interrupting him, said, "But you really must have been out of your senses to fasten yourself on me, who am myself always accustomed to fasten upon others."

It is folly to expect aid and comfort from those who have habitually wrought us mischief.

The Raven and the Swan

A Raven envied a Swan the whiteness of her plumage, and, thinking that its beauty was owing to the water in which she lived, he deserted the highest branches where he used to find his livelihood, and betook himself to the pools and streams. There he plumed and dressed himself and washed his coat, but all to no purpose, for his plumage remained as black as ever, and he himself soon perished for want of his usual food.

Change of scene is not change of nature.

The Fisherman Piping

A Man who cared more for his music than his nets, on seeing some fish in the sea, began playing on his pipe, thinking that they would jump out on shore. But finding himself disappointed, he took a casting net, and, enclosing a great multitude of fish, drew

172

them to land. When he saw the fish dancing and flapping about, he smiled and said, "Since you would not dance when I piped, I will have none of your dancing now."

It is a great art to do the right thing at the right season.

The One-Eyed Doe

A Doe that had but one eye, used to graze near the sea, and in order that she might be the more secure from attack, she kept her eye towards the land against the approach of the hunters, and her blind side towards the sea, from whence she feared no danger. But some sailors, rowing by in a boat and seeing her, aimed at her from the water and shot her. At her last gasp, she sighed to herself: "Ill-fated creature that I am! I was safe on the landside from whence I expected to be attacked, but find an enemy in the sea, to which I most looked for protection."

Our troubles often come from the quarter whence we least expect them.

The Swallow
and the Raven

The Swallow and the Raven contended which was the finer bird. The Raven ended by saying, "Your beauty is but for the summer, but mine will stand many winters."

Durability is better than show.

The Wolf and the Lamb

As a Wolf was lapping at the head of a running brook, he spied a stray Lamb paddling, at some distance, down the stream. Having made up his mind to seize her, he bethought himself how he might justify his violence. "Villain!" said he, running up to her, "How dare you muddle the water that I am drinking?" "Indeed," said the Lamb humbly, "I do not see how I can disturb the water, since it runs from you to me, not from me to you." "Be that as it may," replied the Wolf, "it was but a year ago that you called me many ill names." "Oh, Sir!" said the Lamb, trembling, "A year ago I was not born." "Well," replied the Wolf, "if it was not you, it was your father, and that is all the same; but it is no use trying to argue me out of my supper," and without another word he fell upon the poor helpless Lamb and tore her to pieces.

A tyrant can always find plenty of excuses for his wicked deeds.

The Gull and the Kite

A Gull had pounced upon a fish, and in endeavoring to swallow it got choked, and lay upon the deck for dead. A Kite who was passing by and saw him, gave him no other comfort than: "It serves you right, for what business have the fowls of the air to meddle with the fish of the sea?"

The Fox and the Grapes

A Fox, just at the time of the vintage, stole into a vineyard where the ripe sunny Grapes were trellised in most tempting show. He made many a spring and a jump after the luscious prize; but, failing in all his attempts, he muttered as he retreated, "Well! What does it matter! The Grapes are undoubtedly sour!"

The Boasting Traveller

A Man who had been travelling in foreign parts, on his return home was always bragging and boasting of the good feats he had accomplished in different places. In Rhodes, for instance, he said he had taken such an extraordinary leap that no man could come near him, and he had witnesses there to prove it. "Possibly," said one of his hearers; "but if this be true, just suppose this to be Rhodes, and try the leap again."

The Wild Ass
and the Lion

A Wild Ass and a Lion entered into an alliance that they might capture the beasts of the forest with greater ease. The Lion agreed to assist the Wild Ass with his strength, while the Wild Ass gave the Lion the benefit of his greater speed. When they had taken as many beasts as their necessities required, the Lion undertook to distribute the prey, and for this purpose divided it into three shares. "I will take the first share," he said, "because I am King, and the second share, as a partner with you in the chase. The third share, believe me, will be a source of great evil to you, unless you willingly resign it to me, and set off as fast as you can." And so he did.

Might makes right.

The Travellers
and the Hatchet

Two Men were travelling along the same road, when one of them, picking up a hatchet cries, "See what I have found!" "Do not say *I,*" says the other, "but *we* have found." After a while, up came the men who had lost the hatchet, and charged the man who had it with the theft. "Alas," says he to his companion, "we are undone!" "Do not say *we,*" replies the other, "but *I* am undone; for he that will not allow his friend to share the prize, must not expect him to share the danger."

The Swallow
in Chancery

A Swallow had built her nest under the eaves of a court of Justice. Before her young ones could fly, a Serpent gliding out of his hole ate them all up. When the poor bird returned to her nest and found it empty, she began a pitiable wailing. But a neighbor suggested by way of comfort that she was not the first bird who had lost her young. "True," she replied, "but it is not only my little ones that I mourn, but that I should have been wronged in that very place where the injured fly for Justice."

The Fowler
and the Viper

A Fowler, taking his birdlime and his twigs, went out to catch birds. Seeing a thrush sitting upon a tree, he wished to take it, and fitting his twigs to a proper length, he watched intently, having his whole thoughts directed towards the sky. While thus looking upwards, he unawares trod upon a Viper, asleep just before his feet. The Viper, turning towards him, stung him, and he, falling into a swoon, said to himself, "Poor wretch that I am! While trying to destroy others, I myself have fallen unawares into the snares of death."

The Vain Wolf
and the Lion

A Wolf, roaming by the mountain's side, saw his own shadow, as the sun was setting, become greatly extended and magnified, and he said to himself, "Why should I, being of such an immense size, and extending nearly an acre in length, be afraid of the Lion? Ought I not to be acknowledged as King of all the collected beasts?" While he was indulging in these proud thoughts, a Lion fell upon him, and killed him. He exclaimed with a too late repentance, "Poor fool that I was! By thinking too well of myself I have brought about my own destruction."

The Fox and the Lion

A Fox who had never seen a Lion, when by chance
he met him for the first time, was so terrified that he
almost died of fright. When he met him the second
time, he was still afraid, but managed to disguise his
fear. When he saw him the third time, he was so
much emboldened that he went up to him and asked
him how he did.

Familiarity breeds contempt.

The Fox and the Crow

A Crow had snatched a goodly piece of cheese out
of a window, and flew with it into a high tree, intent
on enjoying her prize. A Fox, passing under the tree,
spied the dainty morsel, and determined to have it
for himself. "Oh, Crow," he said, "how beautiful
are your wings, and how bright your eyes! How
graceful is your neck, and your breast is the breast of

an Eagle! What a terrible pity that such a bird should lack a voice to match its greatness of form." The Crow, pleased with this flattery, was determined to prove the Fox mistaken, and opened her beak to give out a loud caw. As soon as she did so, down dropped the cheese! The Fox snapped it up as soon as it touched the ground, and when he had finished eating it he observed, "While your beauty is certain, your brains are meager indeed."

Men seldom flatter without some private end in view. Those who listen to such music may expect to pay the piper.

The Horse
and the Groom

A Groom used to spend whole days in currycombing and rubbing down his Horse, but at the same time stole his oats, and sold them for his own profit. "Alas!" said the Horse, "if you really wish me to be in good condition, you should groom me less, and feed me more."

The Man
and His Two Wives

In days when a man was allowed more wives than one, a middle-aged bachelor, who could be called neither young nor old, and whose hair was only just beginning to turn gray, fell in love with two women at once, and married them both. The one was young and blooming, and wished her husband to appear as youthful as herself; the other was somewhat more advanced in age, and was as anxious that her husband should appear a suitable match for her. So, while the young one seized every opportunity of pulling out the good man's gray hairs, the old one was as industrious in plucking out every black hair she could find. For a while the man was highly gratified by their attention and devotion, till he found one morning that, between the one and the other, he had not a hair left.

Those who seek to please everybody end by pleasing nobody.

The Shepherd
and the Sheep

A Shepherd driving his Sheep to a wood, saw an oak of unusual size, full of acorns, and, spreading his cloak under the branches, he climbed up into the tree, and shook down the acorns. The Sheep, eating the acorns, inadvertently frayed and tore the Shepherd's cloak. The Shepherd, coming down and seeing what was done, said, "O you most ungrateful creatures! You provide wool to make garments for all other men, but you destroy the clothes of him who feeds you."

The Blackamoor

A certain man bought a Blackamoor, and thinking that the color of his skin arose from the neglect of his former master, he no sooner brought him home than he procured all manner of scouring apparatus, scrubbing brushes, soaps, and sandpaper, and set to work with his servants to wash him white again. They drenched and rubbed him for many an hour, but all in vain. His skin remained as black as ever, while the poor wretch all but died from the cold he caught during the operation.

What is bred in the bone will stick to the flesh.

The Kingdom of the Lion

The beasts of the field and forest had a Lion as their King. He was neither wrathful, cruel, nor tyrannical, but just and gentle as a King should be. He made during his reign a royal proclamation for a general assembly of all the birds and beasts, and drew up conditions for a universal league, in which the Wolf and the Lamb, the Panther and the Kid, the Tiger and the Stag, the Dog and the Hare, should live together in perfect peace and amity. The Hare said, "Oh, how I have longed to see this day, in which the weak shall take their place with impunity by the side of the strong."

The Lamb and the Wolf

A Lamb pursued by a Wolf took refuge in a temple. Upon this the Wolf called out to him, and said that the priest would slay him if he caught him. "Be it so," said the Lamb: "It is better to be sacrificed to God, than to be devoured by you."

The Bundle of Sticks

A Husbandman who had a quarrelsome family, after having tried in vain to reconcile them by words, thought he might more readily prevail by an example. So he called his sons and bade them lay a bundle of sticks before him. Then, having tied them into a faggot, he told the lads, one after the other, to take it up and break it. They all tried, but tried in vain. Then, untying the faggot, he gave them the sticks to break one by one. This they did with the greatest ease. Then said the father, "Thus you, my sons, as long as you remain united, are a match for all your enemies; but differ and separate, and you are undone."

Union is strength.

INDEX

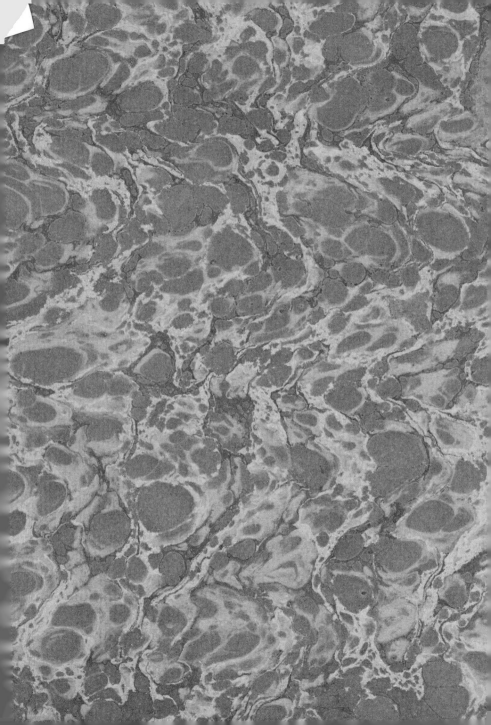